Indian Mythology

Indian Mythology

Tales, Symbols, and Rituals
from the Heart
of the Subcontinent

Devdutt Pattanaik

Inner Traditions
Rochester, Vermont

Inner Traditions International
One Park Street
Rochester, Vermont 05767
www.InnerTraditions.com

Library of Congress Cataloging-in-Publication Data

Pattanaik, Devdutt.
  Indian mythology : tales, symbols, and rituals from the heart of the Subcontinent / Devdutt Pattanaik.
    p. cm.
Includes bibliographical references and index.
  ISBN 978-0-89281-870-9
  1. Mythology, Hindu. I. Title.
  BL2001.3.P37 2003
  294.5'13—dc21

                              2003000048

Printed and bound in the United States

10 9

Text design and layout by Rachel Goldenberg
This book was typeset in Veljovic and Avenir

Contents

∻ *Introduction* ∻
Constructing Hindu Myth

*C*onsider this: A religion believes in one god, who is the all-powerful God, and in one life and one way of living one's life—by obeying the will of that god, as expressed through a prophet—in order to gain everlasting joy in heaven after death. The alternative is to face eternal suffering in hell.

Now consider this: Another religion believes there are several gods, even Gods and Goddesses, several lifetimes, and several ways of living one's life. This religion has no need for the concept of evil because every event is a reaction to past events. This religion maintains that there are several "heavens" and several "hells," where gods can be punished and demons worshipped. This religion holds that the cosmos is multilayered and populated by a variety of beings, and believes that time is cyclical, with events repeating themselves again and again and again.

It would be foolish to try to understand one religion in terms of the other. Hence, to understand Hindu mythology—its sacred narratives, art, and ritual—a paradigm shift is required. One must move away from Western concepts of right/wrong,

1

divine/diabolical, angel/sinner, heaven/hell, genesis/apocalypse, and fall/return. These concepts evolved to satisfy the needs of the Occident, and they presently form the bedrock, in some form or other, of Judaism, Christianity, and Islam. In India a different worldview evolved over four thousand years, with the concepts responding to various sociocultural phenomena and transforming with the words of wise men to satisfy the needs of the local population. European scholars who were deeply influenced by biblical thought defined this worldview as a religion. For the native practitioners it was simply a way of life into which one was born.

European colonial powers were confronted with the Hindu way of life when mercantile and later imperial ambitions brought them to South Asia in the sixteenth century. By the middle of the nineteenth century the Indian subcontinent had become part of the British Raj. India had been under foreign rule before: Persians, Greeks, Huns, Turks, and Mongols all governed the land. But the earlier invaders had either been assimilated into the local population or had left the natives alone, calling those who stubbornly refused to convert to their ways "nonbelievers." The European rulers, however, kept a self-conscious distance from the conquered race and made concerted efforts to understand them. They knew that the secret of political control lay in a sound knowledge of the subjects.

The British, and to some extent the French and Portuguese, soon realized that understanding the dominant religion of India was nothing short of solving a conundrum. There was no historical founder or prophet (like Jesus or Muhammad), no well-defined god (like Jehovah or Allah), no sacred book (like the Bible or the Koran). The translations of sacred texts revealed no clear sense of history or geography. The traditions were varied. There was no clear difference between the sacred and the secular, no consistency between philosophy and practice. In short, there was no "religion." The British needed to construct a religious entity to make the complex beliefs and practices of the conquered people comprehensible. They needed Hinduism.

The Persians and later the Arabs had used the word *Hind* or *Hindostan* to describe the land around and beyond the river that was known to the Greeks as the Indus and to the local population as the Sindhu. In the sixteenth century, Sanskrit and Bengali texts used the word *Hindu* to refer to locals who were not *Yavana,* or Muslim. When the British came to India, they used the word *Hindoo* or *Hindu* rather loosely, applying it to all who spoke the Hindi language in North India. Later the word was used specifically for that segment of Indian population who did not identify themselves as Muslim, Sikh, Jain, or Christian. In the early part of the nineteenth century *Hinduism* became an umbrella term for a number of distinct South Asian sects and regional religions that shared certain fundamental beliefs, ritual practices, and cultural symbols. More specifically, in 1830 scholars used the term for the religion of high-caste brahmanas, which in academic circles is now termed *Brahmanism* and is viewed as a dominantly pervasive subset of Hinduism.

Brahmanism was the only coherent religious system that the British could identify within the Hindu framework. This system was common to the entire subcontinent and had its own literature, written in Sanskrit, a language that European philologists were convinced was the root of all modern European languages. But nineteenth-century Europe was a formidable imperial force and was in the throes of the Enlightenment. It was a world where things were "right" and "real" only if they were logical or scientific. Scientific methodology demanded documented evidence, coherent translations, and objective analysis. This analysis was applied to Brahmanical scriptures, and soon the reconstruction of India's past gathered momentum in European universities for the benefit of the colonial powers.

The Brahmanical texts were classified into two groups: the

Veda (believed by natives to be *shruti,* or revelation) and the
Shastra (*smriti,* or tradition). The Veda captured lofty philosophies and leaned toward logic and monotheism. The Shastra, on
the other hand, supported social customs including idol worship
(condemned in the Bible) and the caste hierarchy (distasteful in
view of the liberal political philosophies emerging in Europe).
Thus, like Al Beruni, a tenth-century Arab scholar, the Europeans
soon recognized the wide gap between the ideas found in classical texts and the beliefs of the ordinary people. The former, which
were more comprehensible and acceptable to European sensibilities, came to be seen as the "high," "pure," "true," "classical," and
"greater" Hindu religion. The latter were qualified as "low," "corrupt," "fallen," "folk," and "lesser." Lower still were tantric texts
and imagery and the customs of the lower castes that lacked a
scriptural foundation. They seemed more like witchcraft to the
European mind. The classical tradition aroused the orientalist's
fascination with the exotic noble savage. The folk tradition
inspired the white man's burden to civilize primitive India and
justified the missionary's zeal to save pagan India.

Today in the postmodern era the colonial discourse has been
severely criticized, and we realize that the "objective" comments
of "logical and scientific" European scholars were in fact points of
view influenced by imperial standards, which in turn were based
on classical Greek sensibilities and biblical paradigms. Judgments
on "high" and "low" cultures revealed more about the attitudes of
the scholars than reality in South Asia. Unfortunately, the colonial discourse has played a significant role in reconstructing
Hindu mythology for Hindus themselves. It has generated deep
prejudices against Hindu art, ritual, and narrative. It is responsible for transforming Vedic philosophies into "true faith" while
condemning tantric practices and folk beliefs as black magic and
superstition. If one seeks to unravel the mysteries of Hindu
mythology, coming to terms with this problem is essential. Hindu

mythology was not the creation of Brahmanical bards; the stories were spawned in the collective imagination that captured the worldview of a people. These were appropriated over time and codified by the socially dominant brahmanas as well as their opponents, the Buddhists and the Jains.

The first Indians to be exposed to the Western system of education happened to be brahmanas from affluent and influential families. When confronted with the reconstructed vision of their religion that contrasted with the egalitarian political systems that evolved in nineteenth-century Europe, the brahmanas became defensive or apologetic. They led the Hindu Renaissance that would ultimately redefine Hinduism using biblical vocabulary (heaven, hell, god, demon, angel, sinner, prophet, evil, redemption, salvation) in a manner that met the approval of the West. In an attempt to align Hinduism to European and Christian ways, some social reformers went to the extent of establishing Hindu churches. Exposure to the West also inspired practitioners of Indian traditions to make Hindu beliefs and practices more "scientific," and hence "real." This trend is perpetuated even today by a generation desperately seeking to reclaim the past.

Sacred Hindu narratives remain spellbound by European prejudices. The battle of the gods and demons is still viewed as the battle of good and evil—never mind the fact that all scriptures describe the demons as half-brothers of the gods and, very often, morally superior to the gods. Krishna continues to be visualized as a "blue" god (people go out of their way to explain why he is not black) although the word *krishna* means "black" in Sanskrit and there are several vernacular songs in which Krishna asks his mother in no uncertain terms, "Why am I dark? Why is my beloved Radha fair?" The polygamous affections of the gods are either ignored or rendered asexual through allegorical explanations. The nakedness of goddesses arouses shame and outrage. The worship of plants and animals are reduced to remnants of a prelogical past. The cyclical scheme of life is so buried that every new version of ancient lore, be it Ramayana or Mahabharata, is structured linearly, beginning with "once upon a time" and ending with "happily ever after."

This book aims to break free from the demands of colonial logic and biblical prejudice. It seeks to unravel the mysteries of Hindu mythology on its own terms, in the process demonstrating how Hindu narratives, ritual, and art capture the Hindu worldview. In this case, *Hindu* refers to the dominant and common elements of mainstream Indian traditions. The book is divided into four chapters:

- Chapter 1, Mythology: Studying Myth, discusses how Hindu myth is a reaction to and a communication of humans' understanding of nature. It explains how the various narratives, symbols, and rituals generate for Hindus a paradigm that defines perfection in this world and offers possibilities in the hereafter.
- Chapter 2, Mythosphere: Comparing Myth, compares and contrasts Hindu myths with the myths of other cultures.
- Chapter 3, Mythopoesis: Transforming Myth, discusses how Hindu myth evolved over time, gathering layers of meaning in response to history.
- Chapter 4, Mythography: Interpreting Myth, explores the various ways in which narratives, symbols, and rituals can be interpreted.

I hope this book appeals to the scholar and the general reader, to the Hindu and the non-Hindu. By throwing new light on old material, I seek to help everyone appreciate yet another system of ideas that was created by humans to help them come to terms with life.

⟿ *1* ⟿
Mythology:
Studying Myth

In this chapter we shall see how myth emerges from the fight, flight, and freeze reactions of a community to establish paradigms of perfection and possibility for a culture. These paradigms are then expressed through narratives, symbols, and rituals. The symbols, stories, and rituals surrounding Vishnu, God of Preservation, provide a good example of mythology in action.

Vishnu's skin is blue. He has four hands. In one he holds a conch trumpet, in another a discus-shaped boomerang. The other two hold a lotus and a mace. He reclines on the coils of a serpent or rides an eagle. Hindus call him Vishnu, the preserver of earthly order. His image in temples is adorned with silks, gold, pearls, perfumes, sandal paste, peacock feathers, and bright flowers. His rituals are associated with beautiful music, communal dance, and sweet food cooked in clarified butter.

ᘒ Vishnu and the Earth Cow ᘒ
(Bhagavata Purana)

The earth, tired of being exploited by the kings who were supposed to be her guardians, took the form of a cow and went to
her father, Brahma, for help. She wept, showed him her broken
back, and complained of sore udders. Brahma directed her to
Vishnu.

Vishnu heard the earth cow's woes and reassured her with
these words: "I will descend on earth and relieve you of your
burden. You will refresh yourself with the blood of kings who milk
you in greed." Vishnu descended on earth, incarnating as
Parashurama, Rama, and Krishna, and massacred the unrighteous kings and restored order to the world. The earth was
pleased.

To an outsider Vishnu's image, narrative, and rituals may
seem odd, even silly; to practitioners they are enriching and
empowering. The Vaishnavas believe Vishnu to be the embodiment of the supreme divine principle. His blue color represents
the ether that pervades all space. The serpent he rests on represents time, coiling and uncoiling itself with unfailing regularity.
His eagle is the sun itself. Thus Vishnu is the master of space and
time and the lord of light. With his trumpet he blows the breath
of life and warns wrongdoers to return to the path of *dharma,* or
orderly conduct. With his mace he strikes those who do not lis-
ten. The rest are given the bright, fragrant, and dew-drenched
lotus of material joy. Vishnu's discus-shaped boomerang, a lethal
weapon that can decapitate demons, is euphemistically called *Sudarshana,* which means "pleasing vision." It maintains the
rhythm of the cosmos and destroys negativity in perception so
that the glass of life appears half full, not half empty. Vishnu not
only sustains life; he makes life worth living.

When dharma is under threat Vishnu descends from his celestial abode in various forms to set things right. In one of his incarnations, as Krishna, Vishnu is the divine cowherd called Go-vinda or Go-pala (see Fig. 1.1). The cow is the earth itself, whose milk sustains life. In exchange she has to be taken care of. Vishnu institutes dharma so that the relationship of humans with earth or culture with nature is harmonious. The practice of cow worship, the taboo against beef, and, eventually, the vegetarianism that is characteristic of Vaishnava Hinduism probably have roots in these beliefs.

As the Vishnu mythology demonstrates, every spiritual experience, every religious practice, every holy vision is grounded in a very special vocabulary that is indifferent to rationality. This is the vocabulary of the sacred, and it is expressed in and shared through stories, images, and rituals. They nourish the day-to-day existence of the believer.

The nonbeliever finds it difficult to accept this vocabulary as real or reasonable. Tales of virgin births, of creation within seven days, of blissful heavens and fiery hells, of gods who bring fame and fortune, of demons who cause disease and death, cannot be qualified as fact. The image of a woman with four hands seated on a lotus, or a man with the head of an elephant, cannot be taken literally. Customs such as cutting the foreskin to commune with a supernatural force or making offerings in fire altars to appease unseen spirits do not appeal to logic. They may be profound to a people, but to the rational mind sacred stories, images, and customs remain fantastic—even absurd—and are hence branded as "myth."

MYTH AND MYTHOLOGY

Myth can be defined in two ways. First, it is a sacred idea that is inherited over generations. Second, it is absurd, irrational, and fantastic concepts about the world that appeal to unsophisticated minds. The two meanings are two sides of the same coin.

Depending on one's point of view, a story, an image, or a custom can be sacred or stupid. If one believes that only rational ideas are real then sacred ideas are bound to be unreal, because the concept of sacredness—and, by extension, divinity—defies logic. The sacred comes from the realm of faith, not reason, and from mythos, not logos. No scientist can ever explain why a river is holy or a ritual hallowed. No mathematician can ever quantify the value of a chant or the power of a charm. To truly appreciate the magnificence of myth, the logical mind has to suspend its disbelief. The need to explain ideas and events through rationalization has to be abandoned.

A good example of faith-based action would be the fact that all Hindus worship Ganesha at the start of any activity (see Fig. 1.2). He is a corpulent elephant-headed deity with a protruding belly, and he rides a rat. His image is placed on gates and doorways. These practices may seem primitive, pagan, and superstitious to non-Hindus and rationalists. To the believer, however, Ganesha is the perfect symbol of unstoppable power (elephant head), prosperity (rotund body and potbelly), and protection (the rat, which is a pest, has been domesticated and turned into his vehicle). He opens the doorway to material success and spiritual growth. By invoking Ganesha's name when beginning an activity and by placing his image at the entrance of the place where the activity will take place, the devotee ritually and symbolically expresses his or her intention to the cosmos. This elaborate and intense expression is seen as the first step in manifestation and fulfillment of the practitioner's intention.

Of course, to the believer, Ganesha's myth is both real and rational. Any attempt to prove otherwise is met with hostility. The world in which the scientist and the believer live is dominated by the Hegelian maxim "All that is rational is actual, and all that is actual is rational." To the believer who considers every element of his faith to be actual, his beliefs *have to be* rational.

Believers make a narrative sacred and endow it with mythic power. In the secular realm myth may still be fascinating when shorn of its sacred splendor. It will entertain but not empower. It may move a person through his or her lifetime but never bind a people over generations. Without faith these vital elements of culture are reduced to amusing tales, impressive art, and curious customs. When Disney makes an animated film about Hercules, it reduces Greek gods to caricatures without a moment's hesitation; there is no one who will be offended by an irreverent portrait of Zeus or Hera. But Disney has to be extra sensitive when it animates the story of Moses. The sea may or may not have parted for Moses, but for believers it did. And no amount of scientific opinion will have any effect on the faithful.

There are fundamental differences between myth and science. Myth transmits a traditional culture-specific understanding of the world. Science seeks a universal understanding of the world. Myth needs faith, not proof. Science needs proof, not faith. When scientific principles are used to unravel myth, when mythos is understood through logos, the enterprise is known as mythology. Mythology involves:

- Systematic compilation and classification of myth, and the comparison of one mythosphere (sacred ideas specific to one culture) with another
- Documentation and analysis of the myth's transformation over time and space to satisfy different cultural and historical needs (mythopoesis), and speculation on the timeless, universal mythmaking urge
- Interpretation of various expressions of myth (mythography) to discover what they are supposed to communicate and what makes them sacred

Believers tend to look upon such rational exercises with distrust. Science by its very nature is disrespectful: It violates everything through curiosity and question. To find one's most precious beliefs and customs being scrutinized by "reasonable" minds can be quite traumatic. We fear that rationality will demystify myth and explain away sacred ideas. We fear that the logical mind will convince the younger generation that ancient inherited ideas are nothing but valued imaginations, and that God is merely a convenient hypothesis. We fear that analyzing myth, exposing its irrationality, and understanding the foundation of faith will destroy sacredness itself. This fear is not unjustified when we consider how mythology as a subject came into being.

It all began when classical Greek philosophers started to question everything. In their quest for the truth, nothing was accepted if it did not appeal to reason. Ancient narratives of Hesiod—the original mythos—explaining the origin of the gods were rejected in favor of scholarly explanations, discussions, and debates. The philosophers rationalized the Olympian gods and pulled down priests and oracles from their pedestals. The trend began five centuries before the common era, and it reached its climax when the Greco-Roman empire gave way to Christendom and logos was used to explain away the old pagan gods to make way for the new God and his son, Jesus Christ.

Mythology established itself as a subject in European universities during the Enlightenment, not long after seafarers came in contact with the peoples of the Americas, Africa, and Asia, whose beliefs and customs made sense neither to the rational nor the Christian mind. The rationalists felt the need to liberate the mind of the "savage" from the numbing power of superstition. The Christians were compelled to prove the absurdity of false gods so that the "infidel" would willfully turn to the true god of their church.

While scientific logic was applied to the narratives, symbols, and rituals of the savage and the infidel, few scholars dared apply logos to biblical mythos for fear of social backlash. European universities and culture could not reject the Christian legacy. Scholars dared not analyze the narrative of Jesus Christ's resurrection as yet another story of fertility and mystery cults with ideas based in the Orphic and Mithraic traditions, where the death and rebirth of a god reflected the rhythm of nature and the relationship of flesh and the soul. Such analysis would have reduced Jesus Christ to a mere representation, not a reality. This was unacceptable, for the historicity of Christ was unquestionable in the Christian worldview, which saw life on Earth as an unfolding plot that began in Eden.

The world has changed in the past fifty years, especially with postmodernism questioning the very basis of Western science and highlighting the strategic bias in the colonial discourse. In the era of political correctness, the erstwhile colonies demand equal status for their beliefs. But global culture is not quite what we might expect it to be. Today it may be easier to refer to biblical myth and analyze Christ as a sacred symbol, but it is tougher to talk about Hindu myth. All people—not just the white, European, Christian male—take offense at any attempt to brand their sacred narratives, images, and rituals as expressions of myth.

In his incarnation as Rama, Vishnu embodies all that is considered virtuous in Hinduism: discipline, detachment, obedience, selflessness, faithfulness, fairness, poise, and dignity (see Fig. 1.3). His story is told in the epic Ramayana. When the epic is treated as a quasi-historical document, Rama loses his mythic power as the symbol of perfection and becomes a mere king. When the epic is seen as literature, Rama becomes a figment of poetic imagination and loses his spiritual splendor. The tension between Rama the historical personality and Rama the sacred symbol has come to the fore in recent times, as Rama has become part of the nationalist Hindu political rhetoric.

EXPRESSIONS OF MYTH

Myth is all about communication; it is a special kind of communication that establishes a relationship between the macrocosm (universe), mesocosm (society), and microcosm (humans). Communication is established through three avenues:

- Narratives
- Symbols
- Rituals

Narratives, symbols, and rituals that express myth may be seen as the vocabulary of a religion; they construct the communal belief that binds a people. Thus the narrative of nativity and resurrection, the symbol of the shepherd and the crucifix, and the rituals of baptism, communion, and confession bind all Christians. Likewise the narrative of Buddha's enlightenment, the symbol of the lotus, the atheistic worldview, and the ritual chanting of the hymn through which the aspirant surrenders himself to the Buddhist way binds Buddhists all over the world.

For the communication to be an expression of myth, it must be viewed as sacred by both the communicator and his or her audience. The communication must appeal not to a person but to a people. And it must be made in a ritually prescribed manner. Consider, for example, the epic Ramayana. This narrative is reduced to literature unless the reader reveres the narrative and seeks spiritual guidance in it. Its status as a sacred tale comes from the way it is revered by a large number of Hindus, not just one or two devotees. And, finally, the theatrical enactment of the epic in North India known as Ramalila may entertain millions, but it attains mythical status because it is performed only at a particular time of the year during the annual commemoration of Rama's victory over his foes.

The Sacred Narrative

An expression of myth becomes sacred when it is of anonymous origin, a revelation or a communication from a nonhuman source. No one knows who first composed the story of Brahma, who drew the first swastika, who planned the first *yagna,* or Vedic fire sacrifice. This gives myth a sense of timelessness and trans- forms it into a natural phenomenon perceived by the wise, rather than an artificial construct of humans. Though a sacred idea may have evolved organically over years, satisfying different needs at different times and capturing within it various layers of meaning, the believer usually does not attribute historicity to any expres- sion of myth. Historicity is often achieved by attributing the source of a scripture or ritual or symbol to God. In tantric scrip- tures one often finds a guru describing chants, charms, and ritu- als to his disciple, insisting that he learned them from a line of teachers who learned them from Agastya, a legendary sage, who learned it from Nandi, a forest spirit, who in turn overheard a secret conversation between Shiva and Shakti (tantric visualiza- tions of God and Goddess). Likewise devotees of the Koran insist that it is of nonhuman origin because it is a record of the words of Allah expressed to the prophet Muhammad through the angel Gabriel. Thus a scripture becomes a historical document of an ahistorical truth, and hence sacred.

In Judeo-Christian-Islamic traditions narratives become sacred because they are historical. No one is allowed to doubt the historicity of Moses, Jesus, and Muhammad. But their existence is not seen simply as a consequence of sociocultural events; rather, it is the fulfillment of a timeless prophecy. Had there been no Eden, no original sin, no fall from grace, Moses, Jesus, and Muhammad would not have mythic status. Hindus also attribute historicity to mythic narratives. The epics Ramayana and Mahabharata are traditionally considered history, or *itihasa.* This is established by making the writers of the epic participate in the plot, turning them into reporters, not authors, of the story. Valmiki, who wrote the Ramayana, gives refuge to Sita in the forest. Vyasa, who wrote the Mahabharata, is the biological grandfather of the protagonists, the Pandavas. But both Rama and Krishna acquire mythic power only because they are incarnations of Vishnu who walk among humans to restore and maintain order in every world cycle. Thus history becomes sacred when placed within a divine plot.

A sacred narrative needs to be distinguished from a parable (story with moral ending), a fable (story with animals that express human emotions), history (reportage of an actual event), or literature (an individual's fantasy that seeks to entertain or provoke thought). The sacred narrative reverberates with mythic power by attempting to answer the primordial and profound questions of life:

- How did the world come into being?
- How will it be destroyed?
- What is the role of humankind in this world?
- Why is there suffering in the world?
- What happens after death?

Take, for example, the following two stories from the Mahabharata, which involve the same characters.

◌⚬ Renuka's Umbrella ⚬◌
(Mahabharata)

Jamadagni was a warrior-sage skilled in the use of the bow. His wife, Renuka, was so devoted that she would run after every arrow he shot and collect it as soon as it hit the ground. One day, however, she ran after an arrow and did not return till nightfall. She blamed the heat of the sun for the delay. The furious Jamadagni decided to shoot an arrow at the sun. The sun begged for mercy and offered another solution: He gave Renuka an umbrella to protect her from his heat the next time she ran after an arrow.

∾ Renuka's Infidelity ∾
(Mahabharata)

Renuka was so chaste that she had the power to collect water in unbaked pots. However, she lost this power when she had adulterous thoughts after watching a king make love to his wives on the riverbank. Her husband, Jamadagni, ordered his five sons to behead Renuka. Four of them refused. The fifth son, Parashurama, who was an incarnation of Vishnu, raised his ax and did what was needed. As he was pleased with his son's unquestioning obedience, Jamadagni offered Parashurama a boon. Parashurama requested to have his mother back. So Jamadagni restored Renuka to life using his spiritual powers.

The first story is a parable; it informs the reader how to solve problems by adapting to circumstances rather than blaming them. It can also be seen as a short story that attributes divinity to the origin of the umbrella. However, it lacks the mythic power of the latter narrative, which is concerned with social order, marital fidelity, filial obedience, and patriarchal values. The latter narrative transforms Parashurama into a manifestation of God and provides the inspiration for another narrative that projects Renuka as a manifestation of the Goddess. Perhaps that is why the story of Renuka's umbrella is hardly known beyond academic circles.

∾ Renuka's Head ∾
(Yellamma Mahatmya)

When Parashurama raised his ax to kill his mother, she ran and took refuge in a low-caste community in the hope that her priest son would not follow her there. He did follow her and swung his ax again, beheading not just Renuka but also another woman who had tried to prevent this matricide. When Parashurama asked that his mother be restored, Jamadagni gave him a pot of magical water to be poured on the corpse where the head had been rejoined. In his excitement, Parashurama attached the low-caste woman's head to his high-caste mother's body and vice versa. Jamadagni accepted the former. The latter was left behind to be worshipped by low-caste people as Yellamma, the mother of all.

The high-caste head of Renuka is attached to the rim of a basket or a pot and worshipped by peasants in rural Maharashtra, Karnataka, and Andhra Pradesh. The pot and basket, like the low-caste woman, accepts everything that is placed in it. It represents the earth that accepts any seed—unlike the field (domesticated earth), where the seed is chosen by the farmer. Such beliefs no doubt inspired the custom of making prostitutes out of the priestesses of Renuka-Yellamma. These priestesses belong to low-caste communities, are forbidden to marry or settle down, and are trained from childhood to accept the carnal attention of any man and survive on offerings given to the goddess.

Of all the three narratives revolving around Renuka, the last is richest in mythic power. This narrative seeks to resolve the tension between the adulterous wife and the faithful mother, the cruelty of justified punishment and the moral confusion of compassion, the rigidity of the high-caste Hindu and the flexibility of the low-caste Hindu. In Renuka-Yellamma women can project their own traumas from spousal abuse and marital repression. The narrative and the beliefs and customs it contains and inspires bind together a community.

The story of Yellamma is not recorded in any Sanskrit scripture and has only recently been documented by anthropologists.

This does not lower its value. In fact, most powerful narratives are transmitted by word of mouth from one generation to another, not through scriptures. Narration is a powerful organic process that helps people gain a better, deeper understanding of the world. Stories are told and retold informally by elders of the family, while others are told formally by wandering bards, theater groups, and priests during rituals, ceremonies, and festivals. The narration is entertaining, but recipients know that beyond the obvious is something sacred that subtly permeates their being, almost unconsciously influencing their understanding of the world. Occasionally the tales are documented. These documented tales are not the origin of sacred lore; they are merely "frozen" retellings (see Table 1).

Sacred Symbols

Some ideas cannot be contained in a story; they can only be rep-resented as symbols. Symbols may be realistic (a conch, a flower, a tree), or abstract (geometric shapes). Unlike signs, symbols are open to innumerable interpretations. This makes them highly potent and capable of transmitting ideas that cannot be captured in word, as in the following story of Navagunjara (see Fig. 1.4).

ལ Arjuna and the Navagunjara ལ
(Orissan folklore based on the Mahabharata)

The great archer Arjuna was once confronted by a beast that was a composite of nine animals: He had the head of a rooster; the neck of a peacock; the back of a bull; the waist of a lion; the feet of an elephant, a human, a deer, and a tiger; and a serpent for a tail. At first Arjuna was terrified by this strange beast and raised his bow to shoot it. But then he was fascinated by his inability to identify it or explain the beast's existence. It was beyond all known definitions; it challenged conventional classification. It seemed to emerge from beyond the limits of human comprehension. Arjuna

TABLE 1. COMMON SOURCES OF SACRED NARRATIVES IN HINDUISM

Scripture	Contents	Approximate Date of Origin
Mantra Samhita	Vedic chants that occasionally presuppose a narrative	2000–1500 B.C.E.
Brahmana	Ritual manuals that sometimes offer narrative explanations for a particular practice	1000–800 B.C.E.
Upanishad	Philosophical discourses that are often captured within a narrative structure	800–500 B.C.E.
Itihasa (Ramayana, Mahabharata)	Epics of kings within a framework of divine activity involving gods and sages	300 B.C.E.–A.D. 300 (Sanskrit compilation), A.D. 1300–2000 (folk retellings)
Purana	Chronicles of gods, kings, and sages; some, known as Sthala Purana, are parochial and limited to a particular shrine	A.D. 500–1500 (Sanskrit compilation), A.D. 1300–2000 (folk retellings)
Agama	Temple texts that contain stories related to the deity, temple, and festivals	A.D. 1000–1700
Tantra	Occult texts that contain stories related to deities, rituals, and discourses	A.D. 600–1800
Mahatmya	Hagiographies of gods and goddesses in Sanskrit and folk languages	A.D. 1300–1900
Bhakti literature	Devotional prose and poetry in Sanskrit and folk languages	A.D. 1300–1700

realized that this was no monster; it was a manifestation of the divine. For what is impossible in human reason is possible in divine thought. Arjuna dropped his bow and saluted this magical manifestation of God.

Broadly, all symbols can be divided into fertility or monastic symbols. Fertility symbols are world-affirming, associated with life-giving ideas, and are concerned with materialistic aspirations such as regeneration, experiencing pleasure, having children, and gaining wealth and power. Monastic symbols are world-denying, associated with life-taking ideas, and are concerned with spiritual goals such as truth, bliss, and immortality (see Table 2).

The god of love, sex, and desire, Kandarpa, is associated with symbols of fertility. His complexion is green like tender leaves and he rides a parrot. Like the Western Cupid, he carries a bow and arrow. The shaft of his bow is made of sugarcane, and he has five flower-tipped arrows to rouse the five senses (see Fig. 1.5). The fish serves as his emblem on his banner. Kandarpa is considered the son of the creator and the sustainer of the universe, and the enemy of the destroyer. He entraps souls in the cycle of rebirth and is a hurdle to the path of liberation. When Hinduism became more monastic, the worship of Kandarpa waned. Sensuality was acceptable in society as long as it was linked to devotion. As a result the symbols of Kandarpa mingled and merged with those of Vishnu and his human incarnation, Krishna, who was the most popular object of devotion. The sugarcane, fish-like earrings, peacock feather, winsome looks, wild flowers, parrots, female companions, alluring music, and sensuous dances on moonlit nights on the banks of a river in a flowery meadow that came to be associated with Krishna strongly evoke Kandarpa. But in Krishna the love god's eroticism is tempered with devotion and yearning for spiritual rather than physical union.

TABLE 2. COMMON FERTILITY OR WORLDLY SYMBOLS IN HINDUISM

Type of Symbol	Symbol	Probable Explanation
ANIMAL	Elephant	Powerful, with no natural enemy
	Fish	Indicative of water, and hence life
	Parrot or parakeet	Has a red beak and a green body, thus exhibiting colors of fertility; mount of Kandarpa, the god of desire
	Serpent	Sheds and renews its skin, like the earth renews its fertility, at regular intervals
	Woman	Sheds her (red) seed involuntarily each month
PLANT	Banana	Does not need to be farmed; every part of the plant has economic use
	Betel leaf	Chewed to relax; suggestive of leisure and sexual attraction
	Coconut	Does not need to be farmed; every part of the plant has economic use
	Grass	Grows back when uprooted
	Mango leaf	Leaf of the plant that bears the sweetest of fruits; adornment of Kandarpa
	Marigold flower	Each petal contains the seed of the plant; adornment of Kandarpa
	Sugarcane	Has sweet sap; shaft of Kandarpa's bow
	Turmeric	Antiseptic; keeps away negative elements

TABLE 2. COMMON FERTILITY OR WORLDLY SYMBOLS IN HINDUISM
   (CONTINUED)

Type of Symbol	Symbol	Probable Explanation
MINERAL	Conch shell	Indicative of water, and hence life
	Red powder or dye	Suggestive of blood and fertility
	Venus	In astrology associated with fertility, femininity, and creativity
	Water	Flows downward, indicating it is earth bound; gives life wherever it goes
ARTIFICIAL	Cloth	Woven by humans
	Mirror	Reflects cosmetic beauty
	Pot or basket	Container of food, water, and wealth
ABSTRACT	Circle	Spontaneous shape of most things in nature
	Five-sided star	Indicative of Venus
	Green color	Realized energy; color of new saplings
	Horizontal line	Suggestive of earth and water
	Red color	Potential energy; color of blood and menstrual discharge
	Six-sided star	Union of upward and downward triangles that represent the male and female reproductive organs

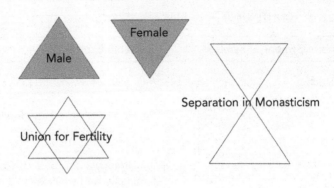

Triangles in Sacred Hindu Geometry

Generally, fertility symbols are associated with water, items that are associated with water (conch shell, coconut), and all things that regenerate rapidly (grass, serpent). Bright (parrot) and sweet (sugarcane, honey) objects also serve as fertility symbols. In contrast, monastic symbols are associated with fire (ash), with longevity (turtle, banyan tree), and with purity and simplicity.

Of course, some symbols, like the lotus, resist such compartmentalization. To the materialist the lotus is the most perfect and alluring transformation of energy; to the spiritualist it is the expression of freedom from the boggy mire of existence (see Table 3).

In one narrative from the Bhagavata Purana, the sage Markandeya has a vision or a dream. In his vision, dark clouds covered the sky. Torrential rains lashed the earth. Rivers broke their banks. The sea tossed furiously. Oceans began to overflow. Terrified, Markandeya sought refuge on a banyan tree. One of the leaves, cradled by the violent waves, caught his eye. On it he saw a beautiful child, radiant like the sun, sucking its big toe, gurgling with joy (see Fig. 1.6). The child inhaled Markandeya into his body. Within he saw a whole new world: celestial regions populated by gods, nether worlds populated by demons, and the earth populated with plants, animals, nymphs, fairies, gnomes, giants,

TABLE 3. COMMON MONASTIC OR SPIRITUAL SYMBOLS IN HINDUISM

Type of Symbol	Symbol	Probable Explanation
ANIMAL	Bull	Lives alone, aloof, untamable
	Man	Can retain his seed
	Swan	Believed to separate milk from water; water does not stick to its feathers
	Turtle	Can withdraw its head and limbs under its shell; has long life
PLANT	Banyan	Long life; gives a lot of shade
	Datura	Grows wild; poisonous
	Hemp	Grows wild; narcotic
	Pipal	Long life; gives a lot of shade
	Rudraksha	Wild forest beads; cannot be farmed
	Sandal paste	Water evaporates and leaves color behind
MINERAL	Ash	Outlives destruction by fire
	Fire	Leaps upward
	Jupiter	Associated with rationality
	Mars	Associated with drive and proactiveness
ARTIFICIAL	Animal skins and bark	Natural fabrics; not woven by humans
	Coconut shell or cranium	Natural bowl; not molded or woven by humans
	Staff	Symbol of authority

TABLE 3. COMMON MONASTIC OR SPIRITUAL SYMBOLS IN HINDUISM
(CONTINUED)

Type of Symbol	Symbol	Probable Explanation
ABSTRACT	Square	Discipline, restraint, order, morality, ethics; artificial construct
	Triangles separated but joined at the tips	Separation of male (upward-pointing triangle) and female (downward-pointing triangle) organs
	Vertical line	Erect; suggestive of uprightness and discipline
	White color	Purity; color of semen

and dwarves. Everything was as perfect inside as it was imperfect outside. The child exhaled, and Markandeya found himself surrounded by the unrelenting cataclysm once again. This time Markandeya faced it with faith, not fear, thanks to the child who lay on the banyan leaf. This image combines symbols of change (water), permanence (banyan leaf), and regeneration (baby). It helps the devotee accept that although change is inevitable, everything regenerates eventually and one aspect always remains permanent: the grace of God.

The most important symbolism in Hinduism is that of man and woman. In most narratives man represents spiritual reality; woman represents material reality. He stands for otherworldly pursuits; she stands for worldly passions. Worldliness is impossible without the presence of women; monasticism demands the absence of women. Man is the soul. Woman is the flesh. He is the cause. She is the manifestation. He is the self, pure awareness, and the true identity of our being. She is the energy, the matrix, in which the self is enmeshed. Since he is the self, he is the subject who experiences life and she is the object who is experienced in life. She owes her existence to him. He owes his identity to her. He creates, sustains, and destroys her. She enables him to preserve, propagate, indulge, and realize himself. Just as man and woman are complementary, so are spiritual and material realities. Hence, when God is represented, Hindus choose not male or female but both male and female. In Hindu temples, therefore, God is always associated with the Goddess. In Vishnu temples one finds Lakshmi. In Krishna temples one finds Radha. In Rama temples one finds Sita. In Shiva temples one finds Shakti. Without either there is neither. The following story from Tamil temple lore illustrates this inseparable pairing of male and female.

ᑕᕑ The Half-Woman God ᑕᕑ
(Tamil Temple Lore)

The sage Bhringi wanted to circle Shiva to demonstrate his devotion. Shakti stopped him, saying, "You must go around both of us, because each of us is incomplete without the other." Bhringi was adamant in circling only Shiva. To foil his plans Shakti sat on Shiva's lap. Bhringi took the form of a bee and tried to fly between them, so Shakti fused her body with Shiva's and became his left half. Shiva then came to be known as Ardha-nari (half-woman god; see Fig. 1.7). Bhringi then took the form of a worm and tried to bore a hole between them.

In exasperation over Bhringi's stubbornness, Gauri said, "If you only want him then may you be deprived of every tissue that a human gets from a woman." Instantly Bhringi was transformed into a skeleton, his body stripped of flesh and blood. He could not even stand. Shiva felt sorry for him and gave him a third leg so that he could stand up like a tripod. Bhringi apologized to Shakti, having realized the complementary relationship between the God and the Goddess.

The symbolism of man and woman is undoubtedly enmeshed in gender politics, with man being the cause and the consciousness and the woman being matter and manifestation. That man represents stillness and the unchanging nature of the soul and woman represents flux and the ever-changing nature of the material matrix says a lot about the Hindu attitude toward manliness and womanliness. But such bias is innate in language. To truly appreciate the idea behind the symbol one has to transcend biology. Only then will the difference between God and Goddess transform into the conflict between individual and environment. Only then will the macrocosmic world of the divine coalesce with the microcosmic world of the self (see Table 4).

Women and fertility symbols play an important role in household rituals such as marriage, childbirth, and harvest. On door-

TABLE 4. DIFFERENT MEANINGS OF MAN AND WOMAN IN HINDU SYMBOLISM

Man	Woman
Culture	Nature
Individual	Environment
Pure consciousness	Energy matrix
Seer	Scenery
Soul	Body and mind
Spiritual reality	Material reality
That which is not contained in space or subject to time	That which is contained in space or subject to time
Subject	Object

ways symbols such as fish, conch shells, and dots are painted in red. Pots filled with water topped with a coconut are placed on a pile of rice. Tender mango leaves and marigold flowers are strung together and hung at the doorway. On the floor just outside the doorway beautiful diagrams are drawn using white and colored powder. Sweet food is cooked in the house. Banana is offered to guests. Married women are invited to the household; they are given flowers, perfumes, gifts, and red powder to apply to their foreheads. Without a wife a man is not a householder. Without a husband a woman is not a housewife. Only husband and wife as pillars of a household are allowed to perform fertility rituals.

ᘓ A Golden Effigy of Sita ᘓ
(Uttara Ramayana)

When Rama returned to Ayodhya after killing the demon-king Ravana and rescuing his wife, Sita, he was crowned king. Rama's subjects, however, did not want Sita as their queen, as she was a woman of soiled reputation. In deference to their wishes Rama abandoned Sita.

As king, Rama had to perform many rituals, but in all of them the presence of his wife was required. Rama, however, refused to remarry; his people had rejected a queen, but he had not rejected his wife. So a compromise was found: A golden effigy of Sita was placed next to Rama as he performed the necessary rituals.

Monastic practices are solitary, involving meditation, austerity, penance, and introspection. Such practice does not need a pair. Monks therefore smear their bodies with ash, wear clothes that are unstitched and colored ochre or white, wear strings of beads, mat their hair or shave their heads, and do nothing to make themselves alluring to the opposite sex or acceptable within the mainstream. In tantric monasticism the ritual does involve a woman, but she serves as a medium or a tool by which to attain the goal. In householder festivals the man and woman work with each other; in monastic practices they work individually, with or without the help of the other.

The pilgrimage to the hill of Sabarimalai, Kerala, is a monastic practice, though it is sometimes performed for very worldly reasons. For forty days the pilgrim has to wear black clothes, eat one meal a day, bathe in cold water, walk with bare feet, and remain celibate, and then he takes an arduous journey through forests to glimpse the celibate boy god Ayyappa, who resides atop a hill. No woman is allowed to enter the shrine. Ayyappa is one of the few gods in Hinduism that does not have a consort.

The elephant-headed Ganesha and the monkey Hanuman are in many traditions viewed as celibate gods, but they are worshipped by women too. These gods are threshold gods, on the border of the material and spiritual realms. Both serve as doorkeepers to the Goddess (see Table 5).

Sacred Rituals

Rituals are choreographed actions through which the believer communicates with the cosmos. The action is believed to have the power to transform the world either objectively (by making divine beings change circumstances in one's favor) or subjectively (by altering perception so that reality changes) (see Table 6).

Rituals bring together the narrative and the symbol. The Christian ritual of baptism or the Judeo-Islamic ritual of circumcision makes sense only when one is familiar with the biblical discourse that man is born in sin and remains in sin until he communes with Yahweh. The Hindu practice of placing red footprints at the doorway pointing inward makes no sense without a knowledge of Lakshmi, the goddess of wealth, whose entry into the house is desired.

TABLE 5. COMPARISON OF FERTILITY RITES AND MONASTIC PRACTICES

Fertility Rites	Monastic Practices
Aim is to harness the abundance of nature	Aim is to break free from the control of nature
All rituals symbolically communicate materialistic intentions to the cosmos	All practices distance the aspirant from the ways of nature
All rituals symbolize sex (offerings of flower, grass, sandal paste, incense) or violence (blood sacrifice, breaking of coconuts, offering and consuming food)	All practices are antisex (celibacy; discarding bright clothes, perfumes, sandal paste, flowers, and jewelry; smearing body with ash) and antiviolence (fasting, vegetarianism)
Appreciate sex and violence as the fundamental principles rotating the cycle of life	Abhors sex and violence, as they bind creatures to the unending cycle of rebirths
Final destination is paradise, where earthly joys never cease even for a moment and where the flesh is immortal	Final destination is liberation from the flesh and the earth, a merger with God, and assimilation with the universal consciousness
Seek eternal material comfort	Seek eternal spiritual bliss
Worldly	Otherworldly

ᕳᕲ Lakshmi's Symbols ᕳᕲ
(Orissan folklore)

A poor woman in the city of Puri cleaned her house one evening, used rice flour to paint sacred symbols on her doorstep, lit incense sticks in the house, and placed a lamp in her courtyard. Attracted by this, the goddess Lakshmi entered the woman's house, and in no time the woman's fortune changed. Wealth poured in. Her cows gave more milk than usual. Her fields yielded more crops. There was always food in her house, no shortage of clothes, and more money than she needed. But then she neglected the house. The symbols disappeared from the threshold, the house was unclean, no lamps were lit, no incense sticks used. Lakshmi was annoyed. She left the house and misfortune returned.

TABLE 6. COMMON TYPES OF RITUALS

Type of Ritual	Purpose	Example
Contagious	Transmitting a desired quality through objects	Collecting leftovers of offerings (food, fabric, flowers, herbs, sandal paste, ash) made to a deity
Invocatory	Calling upon a divine being, saluting and praising him, and compelling him to fulfill desires	*Puja*—offering of flowers, incense, food, and gifts to a god; *japa*—chanting the name of a god repeatedly; *bhajan* and *kirtan*—singing of devotional songs
Social	Facilitating the transition from one stage of life to another	*Samskara*—rites of passage such as childbirth, marriage, funeral
Sympathetic	Repeatedly doing or creating what is desired in the environment	Placing in the house fertility symbols to ensure family prosperity
Transactional	Giving something to the cosmos and asking for something in return; earning good merit	*Havan*—making offerings to gods through a fire altar; *bali*—making sacrifices of animals or vegetables such as coconuts and pumpkins; *daan* and *dakshina*—charity and gifts to priests; *tapasya*—self-denial, austerities, penance

Often a ritual is a composite of different types of rituals. For example, a *vrata* is a common household ritual mostly performed by women, without the intervention of priests, to ensure health and happiness in the household. The ritual is:

- Contagious, involving contact with an object possessing the desired quality, such as the banyan or pipal tree, which symbolize long life, or a full moon, which symbolizes virility
- Invocatory, involving singing songs in praise of a particular deity or reading a story that extols the greatness of the deity
- Social, involving only married or unmarried women who gather around and support each other during the ceremony
- Sympathetic, involving placement of fertility symbols in and around the house
- Transactional, involving fasting, food taboos, all-night vigils, and charitable acts

In the 1970s Hindus were introduced through popular cinema to the goddess Santoshi-ma, who until then was known only to a small community in western India (see Fig. 1.8). The film was a success, and the goddess was wholeheartedly incorporated in the mainstream pantheon. Women everywhere performed the Santoshi-ma-vrata, which involves eating only one meal composed of jaggery and gram on Fridays. Sour food had to be avoided at all costs. The story of the greatness of the goddess was read aloud. The reason for this easy assimilation was that the ritual to please the satisfaction-bestowing goddess involved symbols long associated with fertility. Sweet food, gram, and Friday have always been associated with Lakshmi, the goddess of fortune, while sour food has always been associated with Alakshmi, the goddess of misfortune. Reading the story that glorifies the goddess is a common form of invocation in vrata rituals.

In some rituals, the ritual is more powerful than the gods; hence all that is required is their mechanical execution to get the desired result (as in case of the Vedic fires sacrifice known as *yagna*). In others the ritual is merely a means for communicating with the gods; the intention matters more than the ritual itself (as in the case of the post-Vedic ritual known as *puja,* which involves adoring a deity with flowers, incense, gifts, and food). In the former, ritual purity matters more than moral purity. In the latter, moral purity matters more than ritual purity.

THE FUNCTION OF MYTH

Myth constructs a worldview for a people. It serves as a looking glass through which life comes to order. In other words it constructs a paradigm so that the apparently chaotic world comes to possess a structure. Every culture has its own set of sacred narratives, symbols, and rituals to condition the mind of its people and make them look at the world in a particular way. In this way every culture distinguishes itself from the rest by having its own paradigm.

With a paradigm comes the idea of perfection: what is right and what is wrong, what is good and what is bad. This discrimination establishes a hierarchy in the material world between the desirable and the undesirable. Also, with paradigm comes possibility, a vision of the spiritual horizon.

Two of the most common paradigms are the linear and the cyclical. In the former there is one life followed by an eternal hereafter. In the latter life follows death endlessly. For the Egyptians the hereafter was the land of Osiris, for Greeks it was the Elysian fields, for Vikings it was the hall of Asgard, for the Mesopotamians it was the "land of dust" mentioned in the Epic of Gilgamesh, for Christians it is Paradise, and for Muslims it is Jannat, the abode of Allah. The attitude of a person who believes there is only one life and only one chance is bound to be different from a person who believes that every living being has past and future lives. For a Christian missionary who believes that life is the only chance one has to be "saved," the sense of urgency in his or her mission is natural. But for a Buddhist who believes that there is always another life to redeem oneself, and for a Jain who believes that things happen by predestination, this urgency makes little sense.

The linear paradigm of one life and an eternal afterlife is found in Judaism, Christianity, Islam, and in many ancient Occidental cultures including those of Egypt, Scandinavia, Mesopotamia, Greece, Rome, and Persia. The cyclical paradigm has influenced Asian cultures such as those of India, China, and Japan and forms the foundation of Hindu, Buddhist, and Jain ways of thinking (see Table 7).

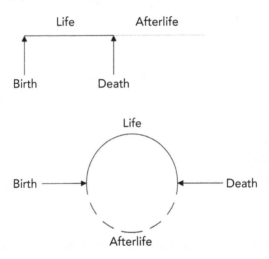

Linear and Cyclical Paradigm

In both the linear and cyclical worldviews, life here and now is imperfect. But the reasons are different. In the linear view life is imperfect because the gods will it to be so (Greek, Assyro-Babylonian), because humans disobeyed God (Judaic, Christian,

TABLE 7. COMPARISON OF WORLDVIEWS

	Judeo-Christian-Islamic	Hindu-Buddhist-Jain
PARADIGM (CONSTRUCTED WORLDVIEW)	Life is made up of one life span, and its problems are the result of transgressing divine law	Death is followed by rebirth, and in life everything changes, with each change determined by past actions
PERFECTION (IN MATERIAL TERMS)	Obedience of divine law revealed through a prophet	Following laws that ensure cosmic rhythm and social order
POSSIBILITY (IN SPIRITUAL TERMS)	Returning to the primal perfection	Breaking free from the cycle of rebirths or gaining mastery over it

Islamic), because an evil one introduced pollution (Manichaean, Zoroastrian), or because humans are the unwitting participants in a great cosmic battle (Norse, Egyptian). In the cyclical view life is imperfect because corruption is a function of time (deterministic approach) or because present events are the direct consequences of past actions (existentialist approach). The possibility offered in some of the cultures that follow the linear paradigm, mainly Judeo-Christian-Islamic and Zoroastrian, is a return to primal purity by obeying the will of God and by fighting the evil one. The possibility offered in Asian traditions is twofold: breaking the endless cycle of rebirths or gaining control over it, and in essence becoming one with God.

Hindus belong to the cyclical paradigm. Known as *samsara*, this paradigm is the material world, the world of death and rebirth. It is nature. It is the world perceived by the five senses and analyzed by the mind. In essence it is nothing but energy. Meaning and value have been imposed on it by a mind deluded by the ego, memories, prejudices, and desires. In samsara nothing is still, nothing is impossible, and nothing is spontaneous.

Every event is an impersonal reaction to the past. This is the law of *karma* that governs samsara. The creator of this paradigm is Brahma, hence samsara is also called *Brahmanda,* or "Brahma's sphere."

In stories Brahma's creation is described as resulting from a woman called Shatarupa, or "she of myriad forms." The name and the female form indicate that she embodies material reality. She is merely Brahma's "observation." Since observation has no existence independent of the observer, Brahma is Shatarupa's creator and father. He is the subject who experiences life; she is a subjective phenomenon, the object that is experienced in life. She exists only to help him answer the question, Who am I? When the question is answered there is no need to observe, and no need for the observation. The observer is self-contained. He shuts his eyes and goes to sleep. The cosmos dissolves. It is *pralaya.*

Pralaya is the cosmic inertia that results when matter is not manifest. This does not mean that matter does not exist during pralaya. In Hinduism creation is not *ex nihilo,* out of nothingness, as in the biblical paradigm. When the spirit is self-contained, insensitive to experience, matter is not observed. In Hindu metaphysics things exist only when they are observed. Hence, unobserved material reality remains uncreated. Creation is sparked when Brahma observes. Brahma observes to answer the question, Who am I? This question crops up as soon as he becomes aware of himself. Just as one is not aware of one's own self in a deep dreamless slumber, the cosmos is not aware of itself during pralaya. This state of nonawareness is nonexistence. Then the spirit awakens. Awareness stirs. The question reemerges. The quest for the answer resumes, and material reality manifests itself once more as the daughter of the creator, Brahma.

Just as dead people are reborn, just as sleeping beings awaken, the cosmos comes to life after pralaya. The cosmic life span is known as *kalpa,* and it is comprised of four eras, or *yugas,* which represent the childhood, youth, maturity, and senility of

TABLE 8. FOUR ERAS THAT MAKE UP A COSMIC LIFE SPAN

	Quarter	Yuga	Phase of the Cosmos	Reproductive Activity	Means to Acquire Wealth	Number of Legs the Bull of Dharma Has
KALPA	First	Krita	Childhood	Thought	Charity	Four
	Second	Dvapara	Youth	Touch	Force	Three
	Third	Treta	Maturity	Intercourse	Trickery	Two
	Fourth	Kali	Senility	Perverted	Exploitation	One
PRALAYA			Death	Non-existence		

the cosmos. Like all material things, the cosmos must submit to time and transform (see Table 8).

The rhythmic nature of both macrocosmic and microcosmic life is driven home by the following narrative.

∾ Rama's Ring ∾
(Folklore based on the Ramayana)

At the appointed hour, it was time for Rama to die. But Yama, the god of death, could not enter his city, as Hanuman, the mighty monkey, guarded it. To distract Hanuman and to let nature take its course, Rama dropped his ring into a crack on the floor and asked Hanuman to fetch the ring. The crack led Hanuman to a subterranean realm where he found countless copies of Rama's ring. The guardian of the subterranean realm explained, "Whenever a ring falls here, a monkey follows it and we know it is time for Rama to die. Such rings have fallen from above for as long as I can remember, and will continue to do so in the future. As long as the wheel of existence rotates, old worlds die and new ones are reborn."

Not only does the cycle of life rotate endlessly, but also each rotation is countless copies of the previous one. The magnitude of samsara is established in the following narrative.

ᴄᴏ A Palace for Indra ᴄᴏ
(Brahmavaivarta Purana)

Indra asked his architect, Vishwakarma, to build him a palace that would befit his status as king of the gods. Every time Vishwakarma completed his construction, Indra demanded that it be made grander. Nothing seemed to satisfy him. Vishwakarma begged Brahma to help. Brahma invoked Vishnu, who took the form of a boy and went to Indra's palace. Indra welcomed his guest and asked him the purpose of his visit. "To see if your palace is better than the palace of the Indra before you," answered the boy. "The Indra before me? Am I not the only one?" Indra asked, perplexed. The boy replied, "Oh, no. There were many Indras before you, and there will be many after you. In fact, at this very moment there are numberless Indras in numberless parallel worlds. One might say you are but a grain on the beach of Indras. When you blink a human dies. When Brahma blinks an Indra dies. When Vishnu blinks a Brahma dies. And when Shiva blinks a Vishnu dies."

Knowledge of his insignificance in the cosmic scheme of things humbled Indra. He stopped making his palace grander. He knew that no matter how hard he tried there would always be someone who was better than he. If there were Indras before him, if there were going to be Indras after him, if countless Indras existed in the present, then what was unique about him? Who was he, really? Indra then became sensitive to life and began his quest to know his true identity.

A paradigm that is endless, boundless, and infinitely repetitive reduces the significance of any particular event. Nothing is unique. Everything that has happened has happened before and will continue to happen again. All happenings are destined. There is no point attempting to control or modify them. It is also foolish to judge them, since all that occurs in Brahma's paradigm is a manifestation of the divine and a reaction to the past. Therefore, nothing is unnatural, unholy, or evil. Everything has a cause, and the ultimate cause is God. Value judgments are thus creations of humans, not ordained by nature or God. Morality and ethics have no place in nature. Animals and plants mate and kill to survive. There is no love or hate, just a tapestry of life-giving and life-taking processes. Impersonal sex and violence rotate the wheel of nature. This is best represented in the form of Chinnamastika, the headless goddess who drinks her own blood while copulating with her spouse or while sitting on a couple who are making love with the woman on top (see Fig. 1.9).

Chinnamastika's female form indicates that she is a visual representation of the observation that is experienced in life. Having sex with the woman on top indicates material reality drawing the life force from spiritual reality. Without awareness and action of the subject, the object cannot exist. He has the power to create; she has the power to sustain and nurture. Chinnamastika's violence (cutting the neck) is an act of defense (suggested by the scimitar) and nourishment (suggested by the drinking of the blood spurting from the severed neck). Sex brings about self-propagation; violence ensures self-preservation. The image of the goddess is unabashedly sexual and violent. Her nakedness and lack of modesty in both the sexual and violent acts indicate the impersonality of sex and violence in nature, their only intention being to sustain life.

While Brahma creates the paradigm, the Goddess is the paradigm. As Chinnamastika, the Goddess represents Brahma's paradigm in all its rawness. The totality of nature, the unabashed display of untamed sex and violence, embodied in Chinnamastika is overwhelming. The average Hindu prefers visualizing her as Lalita-Tripurasundari, the beautiful one, who is gentler and more maternal and holds symbols of beauty and fertility. Lalita-Tripurasundari is the acceptable face of the Goddess. This suggests that in all paradigms some things are desirable and some things are not.

Lalita-Tripurasundari, the most beautiful Goddess, like Chinnamastika, represents Brahma's paradigm in all its totality. Lalita means "beautiful," "coy," or "fine." The goddess is fully dressed as a beaming bride, yet not domesticated. She asserts her independence by sitting on various manifestations of God, including Shiva, Vishnu, Brahma, and Indra (see Fig. 1.10). She is often portrayed with a parrot, flowers, and sugarcane, all of which suggest life-giving processes.

Discrimination between what is acceptable and unacceptable, appropriate and inappropriate, and desirable and undesirable in Brahma's world spawns an aspiration for the ideal. Morals, ethics, laws, commandments, and statutes are created to establish "perfection" in life. Thus a culture comes into being. Culture is based on value judgments, on ideas of higher/lower, better/worse, beautiful/ugly, right/wrong, sacred/profane, appropriate/inappropriate, auspicious/inauspicious. Only the part of the paradigm that is desirable is accepted within society; the rest is rejected.

This quest for taming nature and creating society is expressed in rituals that offer the Goddess clothing, cosmetics, and ornaments such as bangles and nose rings. The devotee wants to see the Goddess not in her full manifestation but in an abbreviated benevolent form. The man of society wants Lakshmi, the goddess of fortune, not Alakshmi, the goddess of misfortune. He wants Gauri, the radiant goddess of the field, not Kali, the dusky goddess of the forest.

In art the circle is used to represent Brahma's paradigm, as it is the most natural of shapes assumed spontaneously by everything from a bubble to a planet or a star. It has no base, root, side, or corner; it evokes a sense of totality and seems as all encompassing as nature. The culture based on ideas of perfection is indicated by a square within the circle. The sharp edges represent the value judgment that is missing in nature. What lies within the square is socially appropriate, while what lies without is socially inappropriate. Outside, sex and violence are untamed. Inside, sex and violence are disciplined by the code of dharma.

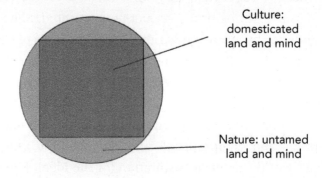

Culture: domesticated land and mind

Nature: untamed land and mind

Circle of Nature and Square of Culture

In the Judeo-Christian-Islamic paradigm, upholding the law of God and demonstrating allegiance to God represents perfection. In the Hindu paradigm, where the world is viewed as being eternally in a state of flux, perfection emerges from actions that stabilize life. Laws that ensure such actions are said to be in line with dharma. Vishnu, the sustainer of the world, institutes and maintains dharma in the cosmos. Dharma brings rhythm in nature and order in culture. Unquestioning obedience of dharma prevents accidents from occurring. All changes become predictable and life more stable. Unpredictable events suggest *adharma,* as in the following narrative.

ᘓ Shambuka Beheaded ᘔ
(Uttara Ramayana)

Rama upheld the code of dharma perfectly. Everything in his kingdom, therefore, moved in a predictable rhythm. But one day a boy died before his father. The father, a high-caste *brahmana*, accused Rama of not upholding dharma in his kingdom. Rama consulted the *rishis*, or seers, who informed him that a low-caste *shudra* by the name of Shambuka was immersed in the ascetic activity known as *tapa*.

The rishis explained, "The world has four ages, just like man—childhood, youth, maturity, and old age. In its childhood only the priest-caste of brahmana is allowed to become a rishi and perform tapa. In its youth, the warrior-caste of *kshatriyas* may also do the same. In its maturity, all except the shudra are permitted to practice tapa. And only in the old age of the world, the era before death, can even shudras join the others in tapa. The current era is the youth of the world. Shambuka breaks the code of dharma by living like a rishi. The resulting cosmic chaos has caused the brahmana boy to die."

Rama immediately went to the forest and beheaded Shambuka. Dharma was reestablished. Predictable rhythms of nature returned.

Order in culture was maintained by the establishment of *varna-ashrama-dharma*, whereby every man was supposed to do his duty (dharma), which is defined by his station in society (varna) and stage in life (ashrama). For women there was only one dharma: obeying the father when unmarried, the husband when married, and the son when widowed. When dharma is upheld perfectly, the rhythm of nature is predictable and no accidents occur in culture (see Tables 9 and 10).

Whenever there is threat to dharma Vishnu incarnates as man or beast to set things right (see Fig. 1.11). Below is a list of

TABLE 9. VARNA: THE STATIONS OF SOCIETY

Varna	Part of Society	Area of Concern
Brahmana	Head	Spirituality
Kshatriya	Arms	Administration
Vaishya	Trunk	Economics
Shudra	Feet	Service

TABLE 10. ASHRAMA: THE STAGES OF LIFE

Ashrama	Aim	Process
Brahmacharya	Preparing for society	Learning
Grihastha	Part of society	Acquiring
Vanaprastha	Retiring from society	Sharing
Sanyasa	Detached from society	Abandoning

incarnations taken by Vishnu through one kalpa. There is no standard list, however; different scriptures offer different lists. For example, in many paintings from southern India, Buddha is not included in the list of incarnations (see Table 11).

Myth, not reality, illustrates perfection. In myth alone does one find perfect warriors, perfect teachers, perfect wives, and perfect sons. Utopia, Camelot, Eden, Dreamtime, and the Golden Age exist only in narratives. Naturally, perfection is something that never exists in the here and now. It always "was" or "will be."

TABLE 11. TEN INCARNATIONS OF VISHNU

Incarnation	Narrative	Period	Evolution
Matsya	Fish who saves the seed of life from the flood of doom	When the old world dies	Fish
Kurma	Turtle who enables devas and asuras to churn the wonders of material existence from the demiurge that defies the natural law of impermanence	When the new world is taking shape	Amphibian
Varaha	The boar who raises the earth from the bottom of the sea	When the new world is taking shape	Animal with four legs but no arms
Narasimha	The man-lion creature who kills the asura who seeks to avoid death, thus upsetting cosmic rhythm	When the new world is taking shape	Half animal, half man
Vamana	The priest who wins the earth for the devas from the asuras through his socially sanctioned right to seek alms	Dawn of the first quarter of worldly life; varna-ashrama-dharma established; kings give alms even if it leads to loss of power	Deformed man (dwarf) who belongs to highest caste and upholds its values
Parashurama	The priest who abandons his socially sanctioned role to kill a corrupt king	End of first quarter of worldly life; caste rules broken; kings begin to steal	Abandons highest caste and adopts the second highest caste to restore social order
Rama	The prince who upholds social values at the cost of personal happiness	End of second quarter; sexual irregularities creep in, with women becoming unchaste and kings turning into rapists	Upholds values of the second highest caste: overpowers barbarians, supports sages, and respects women

TABLE 11. TEN INCARNATIONS OF VISHNU (CONTINUED)

Incarnation	Narrative	Period	Evolution
Krishna	The son of a noble-man who is raised as a cowherd, serves as a charioteer, and subverts the social laws to bring joy and restore justice	End of third quarter of worldly life; caste rules subverted	Adopts practices of lower castes; perpetuates living worldly life, but with detachment
Buddha	The heretic who challenges the principles of varna and ashrama and forges the path to salvation	Fourth quarter of worldly life; rejection of varna-ashrama-dharma	Abandons his caste and rejects family; perpetuates realizing the impermanent nature of worldly life
Kalki	Horse-rider who brings the flood of doom	When the world is old and ready to die	No caste

Eden was; Jerusalem will be. Belief in an imminent utopia helps in dealing with current crises. Thus the idea of the promised land helped the Jews endure for centuries, while the Revelations of St. John gave hope to Christians oppressed by Rome. For Hindus, Rama and his kingdom Rama Rajya represent perfection. He is the perfect son who obeys his father unquestioningly, the perfect brother who selflessly renounces his inheritance, the perfect husband who is forever faithful, the perfect warrior who treats his enemies with respect, the perfect master who treats his servants like equals, and the perfect king who sacrifices personal happiness for his people. His epic, the Ramayana, is therefore read in Hindu households, as opposed to the epic Mahabharata, where ethics and morals are quite ambiguous (see Table 12).

Since the Hindu paradigm is cyclical and everything changes, ideas of perfection also change with time. As a result, for every yuga there is a different "perfect man," or *purushottama*. Rama is

TABLE 12. COMPARISON OF THE EPICS RAMAYANA AND MAHABHARATA

Ramayana	Mahabharata
Story of Rama	Story of Krishna
Appeals to idealism	Appeals to realism
Characters can be easily classified as heroes and villains	Characters resist one-dimensional characterization
Intends to create a civilized society among barbarians	Intends to restore order in an anarchic civilized society
Polished and sophisticated content and style	Crude and primitive content and style
Refers to an earlier age when the world was more ordered	Refers to a later age when the world was on the threshold of disorder
Social and interpersonal values are well defined	Social and interpersonal values are more ambiguous

the perfect man in the second quarter, while Krishna is the perfect man in the third quarter. What is dharma for Rama is not dharma for Krishna. Thus the personalities of the two incarnations of Vishnu are quite different. Rama is august; Krishna is winsome. Rama is straightforward; Krishna is guileful. Rama is monogamous; Krishna is polygamous. Rama is regal; Krishna is charming. Rama follows the rules at all costs; Krishna redefines the rules. Rama is a conformist; Krishna is a maverick. Rama is rectitude personified; Krishna is playfulness personified.

In art, squares within the same circle represent the age of Rama and Krishna. But their orientations are not the same, as what is appropriate in the age of Rama need not be appropriate in the age of Krishna. Appropriate or inappropriate, all things lie within Brahma's Brahmanda.

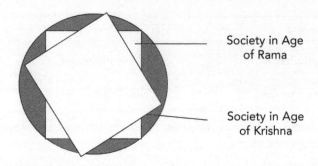

Change in Culture Over Time, within the Circle of Nature

Since perfection is eternally elusive and changes with time, there is a constant search for something that is still, permanent, and unaffected by space or time. Thus the paradigm that generates ideas of perfection serves as a springboard for possibilities. The mind looks at worlds beyond the horizon and at life after death. Blazing visions of heaven enthrall the community. Life becomes more than the empirical. Birth and death no longer limit existence. Ideas of communion (connection with the divine), salvation (rescue by the divine), and liberation (freedom to be with the divine) come into being.

The linear paradigm is sometimes called the triangular paradigm because imperfect life is the result of the fall from perfection, and the possibility offered is one of return—the restoration of primal innocence and purity. In the cyclical paradigm the possibility offered is one of escape from the merry-go-round of births and deaths. The Buddhists call this state *nirvana*, the Jains call it *kaivalya*, and the Hindus call it *moksha*.

Shiva offers the possibility of moksha: destruction of, and hence liberation from, Brahma's paradigm. Release comes when Brahma's question, "Who am I?" is answered. Then the sensory stimuli no longer enchant the mind; all constructs are shattered; perception is liberated from the fetters of time, space, ego, instinct, intellect, memory, and prejudices; and there is self-containment and no urge to act or react. The self-realized subject transcends all needs to interact with the object. Birth and death become meaningless concepts. There is involution into the experiences of *sat* (absolute truth), *chitta* (pure consciousness), and *ananda* (eternal bliss). In other words, the possibility offered by Shiva is not just liberation from the cycle of rebirths; it is also realization of, and union with, divinity itself.

Shiva makes his appearance as soon as Brahma creates a daughter. The daughter is born to help Brahma realize his true identity. Instead Brahma is so attracted by her that he pursues her and seeks to possess her. This incestuous passion is the transformation of the path of self-realization into the path of self-indulgence, the shift of the mind from the eternal, true identity (soul) to the ephemeral, false identity (ego). Shiva appears as an outraged response to Brahma's misdirection and strives to correct it.

⌒ The Beheading of Brahma ⌒
(Shiva Purana)

Brahma saw the first woman he had created, his daughter, and was overwhelmed by desire. The daughter circled her creator with reverence. Not wanting to lose sight of her beautiful form, Brahma sprouted four heads, each facing a cardinal direction. The daughter, disgusted by her father's display of unbridled lust, rose to the sky. Brahma popped a fifth head atop the other four and voiced his carnal intentions. Brahma's mind-born sons howled in horror at the misconduct of their father. From the howl emerged Rudra, who wrenched off Brahma's fifth and most lustful head with his sharp claws. Brahma was thus subdued by violence.

Shiva opposes the creation of Brahma; Vishnu sustains the creation of Brahma. Though apparent antagonists, both Shiva and Vishnu consider the ultimate goal to be moksha. The difference is that Shiva seeks moksha by withdrawing from the paradigm, while Vishnu seeks moksha by staying within the paradigm.

Often something that offers perfection here makes the possible probable in the hereafter. Thus obedience to the commandments of Allah ensures the Muslim divine favor on earth and promises the eternity of heaven in the hereafter. Likewise, upholding dharma guarantees the Hindu peace and prosperity during life and offers freedom from the wheel of existence and union with the divine after death. Vishnu's dharma demands discipline while performing earthly duties. In this way self-indulgence is prevented, and the journey toward self-realization continues. The paradigm is sustained, perfection attained, and possibility realized.

The Mahabharata says that just as the commander of the Pandava army, Arjuna, was about to lead his forces into battle, he lost his nerve and threw down his bow in a moral crisis. He could not bring himself to kill his own cousins, the Kauravas, for a piece of land. His charioteer, Krishna, reminded him of the events that had led to this showdown and tried to motivate him. But Arjuna remained unconvinced. Finally, to bring Arjuna to his senses, Krishna revealed to him the true nature of the world. As this discourse, known as the Bhagavat Gita, proceeded, Arjuna saw the absolute form of the divine (see Fig. 1.12). It was magnificent, with countless heads and limbs releasing the waters of creation and the fires of destruction and containing the terror of relentless time. Friends and foes, kith and kin, good and bad, emerged from God's mouth and were crushed by his teeth. Arjuna realized that his understanding of reality was prejudicial, contingent on his ego, experiences, and expectations; it was not the truth. Having realized that the mystery of life is too profound for the human mind to comprehend, Arjuna detached himself from all judgments, submitted himself as an instrument of the divine, focused on the job at hand, raised his bow, and requested that Krishna

lead him into war. Thus did Krishna show Arjuna how to participate with detachment in the battle of life while staying centered
on the divine.

The divine, which is in essence *sat-chitta-ananda* (truth-
consciousness-bliss), is best represented graphically as a dot or
bindu, that dimensionless entity that forms the foundation of
geometry. Being dimensionless, the bindu belongs to all planes of
existence. Without the dimensionless dot the circumference of a
circle cannot be traced. Without two dots a line cannot be
defined, and hence a square cannot be formed. Moksha is discovering that center, which remains still as the circle rotates and
the square is redrawn. Vishnu's way is to stay centered while
moving with the circumference. Shiva's way is to withdraw from
the circumference toward the center. Vishnu's way is exoteric and
known as *pravritti-marga*; Shiva's way is esoteric and known as
nivritti-marga.

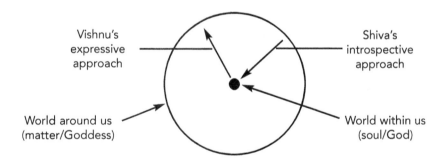

Approaches to Life

The two opposing ways of Shiva and Vishnu are manifest in
imagery, narrative, and rituals. Shiva holds the cranium of
Brahma's fifth skull as his bowl. Vishnu, on the other hand, gives
shelter to Brahma on the lotus that emerges from his navel. With
a glance of his fiery third eye, Shiva kills Kandarpa, the love god

who dares to strike desire into his heart. Vishnu resurrects Kandarpa by assimilating the love god's symbols into his form. While Vishnu uses the axis of space, Mount Meru, and the serpent of time (Adi Sesha) to churn out of the demiurge the wonders of life, Shiva uses them as a bow to destroy three aerial cities of demons that represent the trinity of macrocosm, mesocosm, and microcosm (see Table 13).

Shiva is described as the destroyer because his withdrawal from samsara is destructive; for when spiritual reality does not choose to observe material reality, when God shuts his eye, the Goddess simply dissolves. There is entropy, or pralaya. Brahma therefore invokes the Goddess and begs her to marry Shiva. Vishnu even transforms into Mohini, the enchantress, who seduces Shiva and ensures his transformation from hermit to householder.

Shiva is known as a destroyer for another reason, as well. His asceticism has two forms: Vedic and tantric. In the former he withdraws from society. In the latter he questions every norm of society. In the former he is the solitary ascetic. In the latter he is a dangerous iconoclast feared by conventional society. The Vedic path is known as *Dakshinachara,* the masculine, right-handed way. The tantric path is *Vamachara,* the feminine, left-handed path; unlike in the Vedic way, in the tantric way there is no attempt to avoid the charms of the Goddess or domesticate her wildness. Rather than withdrawing from the world or disciplining our relationship with it, we confront everything that the householder seeks to repress and everything the ascetic seeks to renounce. All taboos are rejected. All rules are abandoned. Sex and violence are embraced wholeheartedly. The senses are roused with heightened stimuli. The body is conditioned with exercises, rituals, and chants to tolerate the stimuli and the journey into the darkest recesses of consciousness. Finally, after much effort, the delusion of the paradigm and the

TABLE 13. COMPARISON OF WORLD-DENYING SHIVA
AND WORLD-AFFIRMING VISHNU

	Shiva	Vishnu
Abode	Meditates on icy mountain-tops, in dark caves, in cedar forests, and in crematoriums	Dances in flowery meadows or reclines on an ocean of milk
Adornments	Serpents and strings of Rudraksha beads	Gold, gems, pearls, and garlands
Attitude toward worldly affairs	Neither incarnates nor participates	Incarnates in many forms to restore world order
Character	Stern ascetic and carefree simpleton	King, lover, and warrior who is guileful and mischievous
Cosmetic	Ash	Sandal paste
Dance	Serene and solitary	Charming and alluring, surrounded by women he beckons with his flute
Drink	Poison and narcotics	Milk, curds, and the elixir of immortality
Earrings	A male earring on the right and a female earring on the left	Fish-shaped earrings suggestive of Kama
Flower	The colorless, perfumeless, poisonous datura	The bright, fragrant, pollen-rich champac
Garments	Covers himself with the hide of elephants, tigers, and deer	Drapes bright yellow silk over his body
Hair	Long, unkempt, and matted	Curly, well oiled
Image	Shiva the ascetic (calendar art, twentieth century)	Vishnu (calendar art, twentieth century)

TABLE 13. COMPARISON OF WORLD-DENYING SHIVA
AND WORLD-AFFIRMING VISHNU (CONTINUED)

	Shiva	Vishnu
In the center of his forehead	Has a third eye aligned neither to the right nor left, indicating unprejudiced discrimination	Has a red mark suggesting acknowledgment of material reality
Leaf	The nonfragrant bilva	The fragrant tulsi (basil)
Musical instruments	Plays the rattle-drum to ward off intruders	Plays the flute to entice people, or blows the conch shell as a trumpet to warn wrongdoers
Relationship with consort	Had to be cajoled and forced into marriage	Has many lovers, wives, and mistresses
Sacred mark	Runs horizontally, suggesting inertia	Runs vertically, suggesting activity
Weapons	A trident to drive away intruders	A sword, a bow, a mace, and a discus

arbitrariness of perfection become apparent. The mind thus becomes enlightened.

With enlightenment comes the power to construct and deconstruct the paradigm. We become one with the creator, preserver, and destroyer. We become a *siddha,* an accomplished soul. We become a *nath,* a master. We become God (see Table 14).

The idea that our concepts of perfection and possibility are the result of paradigms constructed on myth suggests that there is nothing real or natural about these concepts—that our ideas of right and wrong, perfect and imperfect, heaven and hell, here and hereafter, good and bad, are artificial and probably even strategic. These ideas could be either conscious creations or unconscious outpourings of individual or collective minds, but ultimately they remain constructs. And what myth constructs, logic can deconstruct and reconstruct. This makes our concepts of perfection historical and open to interpretation and change. Such reasoning can be quite disturbing and can shake the very foundations of faith, for every truth and every standard becomes contextual. Life becomes devoid of absolutes. Our worldviews become convenient hypotheses. However, it is not necessarily possible to live without myth. The mythless state is also a myth— the myth of the rational mind.

Science may tell humans the how of things but not the why. Why does the sun rise, why is there suffering in the world, why do we all die? These answers can be found only in myth. Myth, not science, can answer the most profound questions of human

TABLE 14. HINDU APPROACHES TO SPIRITUAL POSSIBILITY

Vedic Way		Tantric way
Vishnu's Way	Shiva's Way	
Bridling of senses	Internalization of senses	Arousal of senses
Bestows harmony	Bestows enlightenment	Bestows power
Disciplined participation in society	No participation in society	Rejection of all social norms and conventional morality
Goddess as Lakshmi serves Vishnu demurely	Goddess as Gauri struggles to make a householder of the hermit	Goddess as Chinnamastika displays her full sexual and violent temperament without inhibition
Goddess is Prakriti, nature to be domesticated	Goddess is Maya, a delusion to be unraveled	Goddess is Shakti, pure power

existence: Who am I? What am I supposed to do with life? Why must I do what I am supposed to do? The animal in humans possesses the instinct of sex and violence for self-preservation and self-propagation. The scientist in humans enables them to understand the world. But it is the mythmaker who helps them make sense of it all. Rationality ultimately reduces humans to biochemical entities with personalities that are meaninglessly tossed in a quantum soup. The mythmaker's construct offers the identity, purpose, and meaning that enables humans to self-actualize.

COPING THROUGH MYTHMAKING

Myth, much to the irritation of the rationalist, is an essential component of civilization. Every culture has a myth. There can be no myth without culture. Whenever archaeologists uncover a site of human habitation, they invariably come upon artifacts and monuments that are neither simply utilitarian nor merely aesthetic. These include ritual objects and structures such as charms, talismans, sacrificial altars, temples, and tombs. They make little sense to the outsider, but to the insider they are expressions of profound belief systems that help them grapple with the reality of life. Rational explanations do not adequately justify the time and energy invested in Stone Age cave paintings, Bronze Age burial sites, prehistoric Venus figurines, Egyptian mummies, Aztec pyramids, Stonehenge, the Serpent Mound, and native Australian rock art. The answer to their mystery and magnificence lies more often than not in myth.

Mythmaking is an essential ingredient of civilized life. Through mythmaking humans capture and communicate their understanding of the world. This understanding is crucial in order for people to interact with nature, harness her bounty, withstand her vagaries, and establish a culture where a community can thrive. There can be no culture without myth, because without myth there is no understanding of life.

Fig 1.1. *Vishnu in the form of Krishna, who is Go-vinda, protector of the earth cow (village mural from Maharashtra, twentieth century). More on page 9.*

Fig 1.2. *Ganesha, the elephant-headed god, who is associated with symbols of success without hurdles (Patta painting from Orissa, twentieth century). More on page 10.*

Fig 1.3. Rama, the ideal king, who has become part of nationalist political rhetoric in recent times (Mysore painting, twentieth century). More on page 13.

Fig 1.4. Arjuna and the Navagunjara, a chimerical form of God that defies definition (village mural from Orissa, twentieth century). More on page 19.

Fig 1.5. *Kandarpa, the Hindu Cupid associated with symbols of fertility (Tanjore painting, twentieth century). More on page 21.*

Fig 1.6. *God giving hope to the hopeless by manifesting as a cheerful baby on a banyan leaf that floats on the waters of doom (Mysore painting, eighteenth century). More on page 24.*

Fig 1.7. Shiva as the half-woman god representing union of spiritual and material principles (Kalighat painting, eighteenth century). More on page 27.

Fig 1.8. Santoshi-ma, the goddess who bestows satisfaction (calendar art, twentieth century). More on page 33.

Fig 1.9. Chinnamastika, the goddess who embodies the rawness of nature (Kangra miniature, nineteenth century). More on page 40.

Fig 1.10. Lalita-Tripurasundari, the desirable form of the Goddess (calendar art, twentieth century). More on page 41.

Fig 1.11. Vishnu's ten incarnations from top left to bottom right: Matsya, Kurma, Varaha, Narasimha, Vamana, Parashurama, Rama, Krishna, Buddha, Kalki (Kondapalli toys from Andhra Pradesh, twentieth century). More on page 45.

Fig 1.12. The cosmic form of Krishna containing all things good and bad (Kangra miniature, eighteenth century). More on page 50.

Fig 1.13. Hanuman, the popular monkey-god revered by ritualists, philosophers, and devotees (Mysore painting, nineteenth century). More on page 62.

Fig 1.14. The Hindu trinity of Brahma, Shiva, and Vishnu who create, destroy, and sustain the universe (North Indian miniature, eighteenth century). More on page 71.

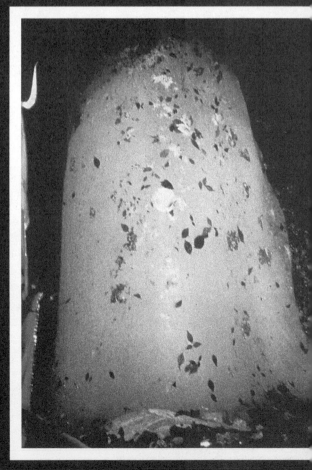

Fig 1.15. The natural rock symbol of Shiva at the Amarnath caves in the Himalayas (photograph, twentieth century). More on page 72.

Fig 1.16. The demon Ravana displaying his devotion for God by creating a lute for Shiva using his own head (South Indian temple art, eighteenth century). More on page 79.

Fig 1.17. The nine deities of Hindu astrology include two demons, two gurus, and five gods (calendar art, twentieth century). More on page 80.

Fig 1.18. *Tuljapur Bhavani, the goddess of the Maratha clan (calendar art, twentieth century). More on page 82.*

ig 1.19. Gateway of a nineteenth-century Vishnu temple in South India (photo-raph, twentieth century). More on page 85.

Fig 1.20. *Details of a South Indian temple wall displaying God as a benign householder, a ferocious being with a lance, and finally a god with many heads and arms (South Indian temple art, eighteenth century). More on page 85.*

Fig 1.21. Yaksha, the forest-spirit who guards treasures (North Indian carving, seventeenth century). More on page 86.

Fig 1.22. Vamana overpowers Bali, who, though a demon, is greatly revered for his generosity (Mysore painting, twentieth century). More on page 91.

Fig 1.23. *Durga
killing Mahisha, the
buffalo demon
(Mysore painting,
twentieth century).
More on page 92.*

Fig 1.24. *Shri, the
embodiment of weal
being churned out o
the ocean by gods a
demons (Tanjore
painting, twentieth
century). More on
page 93.*

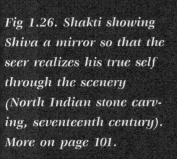

Fig 1.25. A serpent shrine
(calendar art, twentieth
century). More on page 95.

Fig 1.26. Shakti showing
Shiva a mirror so that the
seer realizes his true self
through the scenery
(North Indian stone carv-
ing, seventeenth century).
More on page 101.

Fig 1.27. Saraswati, the goddess of learning and the arts (palm-leaf painting from Orissa, twentieth century). More on page 102.

Fig 1.28. Shiva rescues his devotee Markandeya from Yama, the god of death, thus liberating him from the cycle of rebirths (calendar art, twentieth century). More on page 108.

Civilization requires a state of delusion. We have a need to believe that a culture exists for a reason, that history has a direction, that every event has a meaning, and that every person has a value. Myth provides that delusion. The modern nationalist discourse, which transforms "manmade" borders of nation-states into "natural phenomena," is a case in point. Then comes a tornado or a flood or an earthquake, and all is naught. The flood drowns the kingdom and the republic. Nothing is spared when nature strikes. Both the pig and the priest burn when the earth spits out fire.

To cope with the reality, impersonality, and ambivalence of nature, people turn to myth. Through mythmaking impersonal events have moral or ethical reasons and the faceless environment comes to have a personality. Nature becomes Mother Nature. A father comes to live in the sky. A demon brings disease and death. Somehow it is easier to cope with a mystery that has a face.

Nature is the ultimate reality, existing within and around us. We cannot escape nature. We are helpless. Before nature's awesome capacity to sustain and destroy us, we are reduced to a state of humbling and humiliating passivity. There are three ways to cope with the truism that is nature: fight, flee, and freeze. Each way is valid. At least one is necessary to survive.

She who fights visualizes nature as a force that can be manipulated, controlled, or conquered (one can make things happen in one's favor). He who flees visualizes nature as an enchanting delusion that draws humans away from the true scheme of things (one has to draw oneself away from the enchantment). She who freezes visualizes nature as an impersonal force with a mind of its own (one simply has to go with the flow) or a force under the control of a superhuman entity (one has to pray or petition for events to happen in one's favor). This visualization is mythmaking. No one knows if this process is conscious or unconscious. But it enables the sentient being to cope with life; it makes us human (see Table 15).

In its long history, Hinduism has been dominated by fight, flight, and freeze reactions to varying degrees.

TABLE 15. THREE RESPONSES TO THE CHALLENGE OF NATURE

Reaction to Nature	Nature of the Reaction	Belief	Rituals
Fight	Occult	Nature can be manipulated, controlled, or conquered	Incantations, spells, sacrifices, and charms; rituals are more powerful than the gods and are more important than intellect or emotion
Flight	Mysticism	Beyond the tribulations of nature waits a serene higher reality waiting to be realized	Meditation, asceticism, monasticism, sensory manipulation to lose touch with reality; the mystery of rituals needs to be understood or realized; ritual is secondary to intellect
Freeze	Adoration or appeasement	All events—good or bad—result from the will of a higher power who is either impersonal, and hence cannot be appealed to, or who has a personality that can be adored or appeased	Covenants, prayers, offerings, penance, temples; rituals are an expression of love, allegiance, or devotion and are secondary to emotion

Between 1800 and 800 B.C.E. there was a tilt toward rituals known as yagnas that sought to fight the forces of the cosmos.

Between 800 B.C.E. and A.D. 800, philosophers speculated on the true nature of the universe. They concluded that empirical reality was a delusion and sought to flee from it.

Since A.D. 800 the tilt has been toward theism—to freeze and submit to the will of a higher power who is often given form and enshrined in temples (see Table 16).

These ages, though dated sequentially, are not watertight

TABLE 16. COMPARISON OF THE THREE PHASES OF HINDUISM

	Age of Rituals (Karma Kanda)	Age of Speculation (Gyan Kanda)	Age of Devotion (Upasana Kanda)
TIMELINE	1800–800 B.C.E.	800 B.C.E.–A.D. 800	A.D. 800–present
HISTORICAL PERIOD	Vedic age, before the rise of Buddhism	During the domination of Buddhism	Following the wane of Buddhism in the subcontinent and the arrival of Islam and European colonial powers
INTERNAL TURMOIL	Rise of Brahmanical (Vedic) orthodoxy that is indifferent to the common human and that establishes the roots of the caste system	Restlessness against Vedic ritualism manifesting in Upanishadic speculation; rise of the anti-Brahmanical Shramanas (Buddhists and Jains) whose monastic traditions are open to all; growing popularity of Tantra and yoga among the masses	Accommodation of folk beliefs, tantric practices, and yogic mysticism into the Brahmanical fold; crystallization of Vedic theology; increasing influence of Islamic and Christian beliefs
EXTERNAL INFLUENCES	The Indo-European migration/invasion (?)	Attacks, incursions, and migrations from the northwest by Persians, Greeks, Parthians, Sakas, Huns, and Gujars	Islamic invasion (through central Asia) that establishes the Delhi Sultanate, the Moghul empire in the north, and the Badami and Shahi kingdoms of the south; followed by European colonialism (from the sea) and the establishment of the British Raj

TABLE 16. COMPARISON OF THE THREE PHASES OF HINDUISM (CONTINUED)

	Age of Rituals *(Karma Kanda)*	Age of Speculation *(Gyan Kanda)*	Age of Devotion *(Upasana Kanda)*
POLITICAL SITUATION	Rise of tribal republics or *Janapadas*	Rise of the empires: Maurya and Gupta in the north; Vakataka, Chalukya, Rashtrakuta, Pallava, Kadamba, Ganga, and Pandya in the south	Fragmentation into several Hindu kingdoms (Rajputs in the north; Palas, Senas, and Gangas in the east; Chalukyas, Yadavas, and Marathas in the west; Kakatiyas, Hoyasalas, Vijaynagar, Cholas, Pandyas, and Cheras in the south; Paramaras and Chandellas in central India) that are constantly at war with each other until they are overwhelmed first by Muslim empires and then by the British Raj
DOMINANT SCRIPTURES	Vedic Samhitas (collection of chants), Brahmanas (manuals for performing yagnas)	Vedic Aranyaka-Upanishads (mystical discourses), Sutras (philosophical aphorisms), Shastras (manuals on how to explore ethical, economic, sensual, and spiritual aspects of life), Itihasas (epics)	Puranas (chronicles of gods, kings, and sages), Agamas (temple texts), Tantras (occult manuals), and innumerable vernacular narratives and literature, as well as Bhashyas (commentaries on philosophy and mysticism)

TABLE 16. COMPARISON OF THE THREE PHASES OF HINDUISM
(CONTINUED)

	Age of Rituals (Karma Kanda)	Age of Speculation (Gyan Kanda)	Age of Devotion (Upasana Kanda)
DOMINANT THOUGHT	Through the ritual of yagna humans attune themselves with the cosmos and all worldly needs can be satisfied	Worldly things cause suffering as they are ephemeral; desire for material things entraps one in an unending cycle of rebirths; to liberate oneself from suffering and rebirth one must strive to discipline the mind, control the senses, realize the ephemeral nature of all material things, and eventually renounce them	The supreme divine principle who embodies the cosmos, who is the cause of all things, and who is autonomous of worldly laws has a personality; through his (or her) grace one can overpower the decree of fate and attain material and spiritual satisfaction
PRIMARY RELIGIOUS ACTIVITY	Yagna (offering), Samskara (rite of passage)	Tapas (austerity)	Puja (worship), vrata (household fertility rites), bali (sacrifice)
EXPRESSION OF BELIEFS	Mechanical	Intellectual	Emotional
NATURE OF CUSTOMS AND BELIEFS	Ritualistic	Mystical	Devotional
ATTITUDE	Fight for a better material life	Flee to a better spiritual realm	Freeze to receive grace of the divine

compartments. Ritual, speculation, and devotion have been part of Hinduism in all three ages, but their relative importance has changed over time. For example, Vedic yagnas may not be the cornerstones of Hinduism today, as they were three thousand years ago, but they are still performed in an abbreviated form as havans. Devotional thought can be traced to early centuries of the common era, especially in South India. Speculation continues to guide modern-day rituals and devotional acts

Hanuman is a popular Hindu god whose strength, wisdom, discipline, and devotion are described in detail in the Ramayana (see Fig. 1.13). For a person with a "fight" disposition, Hanuman is the god who will enable him or her to overcome the baneful astrological influences of any planet. For a person with a "flee" disposition, Hanuman represents the perfect embodiment of humility who has disciplined his sexual and violent urges by adopting celibacy and servitude. For a person with a "freeze" dis-position, the monkey is embodiment of devotion who will solve earthly problems and lead the devotee to God.

CONCLUSION

The vital role of myth in culture is best understood by consider-ing a world *without* myth. In such a world nothing is sacred, not even our homes or our bodies. Everything is profane, open to vio-lation. There is no holy river, no promised land, no chosen peo-ple. Nothing is taboo: fathers can eat their children; mothers can make love to their sons. There is no ultimate truth; everything is provisional. There is no perfect society; everything is relative, depending on one's perspective and the standards one chooses. There is no sin, no afterlife, no rebirth, no redemption, no release. There is no motivation to do the right thing—no heaven to attain. There is no doctrine to cling to in moments of crisis, no angel to thank in moments of joy. Without myth, there are no rites of passage, no milestones to mark moments in life, no rituals to tide over during emotional crises.

A myth prevents us from being reduced (as science sometimes does) to biochemical entities purposelessly storm-tossed in the quantum soup. Myth gives us a role in this world and a purpose in life. We become players in the grand scheme of things. Considering the profound nature of this communication, the myth is naturally handled with great reverence as it is transmitted through generations. Any attempt to violate it, not surprisingly, arouses outrage.

Escape from the questioning mind is impossible. Faith, though popular even today, remains for most people the last resort, used when logic fails. In such a world, contrary to popular opinion, scientific study of myth need not destroy the sacred; it can actually enhance it.

The study of myths helps us understand more about our world and ourselves. It teaches us how our ancestors and our contemporaries have given meaning to the experience called life, how they have responded to the challenges posed by life, how they have reconciled the conflicts that form part of existence. It becomes easier to accept and respect other people's beliefs. We learn that the world is different for different people, that, ultimately, mythos and logos, individually or together, aim to make living a worthwhile experience. And that is OK.

❖ 2 ❖
Mythosphere: Comparing Myths

*D*ifferent cultures understand the world differently. Each one transmits its understanding from one generation to another through narratives, symbols, and rituals. The transmission generates a mythosphere—a mythical world populated by beings who enact the perceived realities of a people and with whom humans can communicate through symbols and rituals. The mythosphere of Egyptians is populated by Osiris, Isis, and Horus, who establish a kingdom in the hereafter. The mythosphere of the Greeks is the realm of the Olympian gods, who gain control over the cosmos after defeating the Titans and are forever suspicious of human ambitions. The Chinese mythosphere has a heaven that possesses the perfection the earth lacks, thanks to the perfect bureaucracy of the Jade Emperor. The Judeo-Christian-Islamic mythosphere has the all-powerful Yahweh, his angels, and prophets who help humankind overpower the temptations of the serpent. The Hindu mythosphere encompasses a divine principle that manifests in myriad ways to create, sustain, and destroy the cosmos while helping everyone discover their true selves.

It is interesting to note that what is considered evil in the Christian mythosphere is very often associated with fertility rites in the Hindu mythosphere. What is considered holy in the Christian mythosphere is associated with monasticism in the Hindu mythosphere. For example:

- The red clothes worn by Hindu brides are associated with "scarlet women" in Christianity.
- The white clothes that represent virginity and purity in the Christian mythosphere are associated with spirituality and otherworldliness in the Hindu mythosphere; are restricted to monks, priests, and widows; and do not form part of household rituals.
- The goat, the symbol of virility that is sacrificed to the Hindu Goddess, is the symbol of the devil in the biblical worldview.
- The *yoginis* of Hinduism, who are handmaidens of the Goddess and are wild erotic creatures, recall the witches' coven of the Christian mythosphere.
- The pentagram is the symbol of Lakshmi, Hindu goddess of wealth, and Shukra, guru of demons, and is associated with Venus, wealth, fertility, creativity, and erotic power in Hindu astrology, but is considered the mark of the devil in Christianity.
- Kali, the manifestation of the Hindu Goddess who personifies nature's wildness and its impersonal life-giving sexual processes and life-taking violent processes, is often described in Western literature as the "dark drinker of blood" and is associated with witchcraft.
- The serpent, which is associated with earth's fertility and occult wisdom in Hinduism, is considered a manifestation of the devil in biblical traditions.

These differences may have arisen because sexuality is considered a by-product of original sin in Christianity, while in Hinduism sex is an essential component of nature that needs to be disciplined by culture.

In this chapter, we shall see how characters and plots in the Hindu mythosphere, though apparently similar to themes from other mythospheres, are really quite different.

The swastika is potent symbol that has radically different meanings depending upon the mythosphere in which it is viewed. To the Western eye the swastika is the symbol of Hitler and the Holocaust. To Hindus it is associated with auspiciousness and fertility. No one knows the swastika's origins, but because of the highly influential Nazi discourse on the Aryan race we tend to associate it with ancient Indo-European solar traditions. Hindus believe the word *swastika* comes from *su-asti,* which means "let good things happen." The inner lines are believed to represent rays of light and the four cardinal directions. The clockwise orientation of the outer lines suggests the rhythm of time. The outer lines also represent the four possibilities of afterlife reserved for humans: plant, animal, divine, and demonic. The dots in the spaces created by the inner and outer lines represent the divine spirit present in the four eras that constitute the cosmic life span. Influenced by the postwar anti-Nazi discourse, there is a strong tendency among Hindus to distinguish the Hindu swastika from Hitler's swastika. Hitler's swastika is said to be black and oriented counterclockwise, while the Hindu swastika is painted red and is oriented in the clockwise direction. While the color black and the counterclockwise direction are considered inauspicious in popular Hindu opinion, they are not "evil" in the Judeo-Christian sense of the term. They are not associated with devil worship; they are associated with Tantra, Vamachara, the antinomian path, and occult practices, which although not part of the mainstream are very much Hindu.

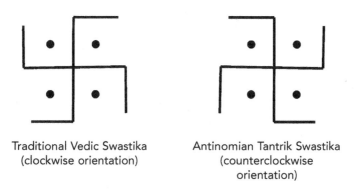

Traditional Vedic Swastika
(clockwise orientation)

Antinomian Tantrik Swastika
(counterclockwise
orientation)

The Hindu Swastikas (usually painted in red)

Misunderstanding of a mythosphere results when words generated in one mythosphere are used to explain events in another mythosphere. The following table demonstrates the different meanings an English word can have, depending on the context (see Table 17).

Words are created to communicate a concept. Since different cultures view the world differently and have different concepts to explain the happenings in their lives, there exist different vocabularies unique to each mythosphere. Some ideas—such as the sun, the moon, food, water, and hunger—may be common to all cultures, but other ideas — such as rebirth, sin, and salvation — may not. The concept of covenant with God, for example, is shared by everyone following the Judeo-Christian-Islamic worldview and is ritually expressed through circumcision and baptism. But the idea is not universal. Hindus have no contract with God. There is no ceremony or act to "bring them into the fold." One cannot become a Hindu; one is simply born a Hindu.

The following table includes words of Indian origin that make sense within the Hindu (and even Jain or Buddhist paradigms) but have no synonym in the Christian paradigm (see Table 18).

TABLE 17. THE MEANINGS OF ENGLISH WORDS WHEN USED IN
DIFFERENT CONTEXTS

Term	Meaning in the Judeo-Christian-Islamic Paradigm	Meaning in the Hindu Paradigm
Demon	Evil being who opposes God	Being who lives underground in bejeweled cities, fights gods, and possess the secret of rejuvenation
God	Creator of the world who banished humans from paradise for their transgressions, who reveals his law through his prophet or son, who will take humans back into paradise if they obey his law and/or accept his son as their savior	Ultimate divine principle, simultaneously impersonal (unmanifest) and personal (manifest), the root of spiritual (symbolized as male) and material (symbolized as female) realities who embodies everything in the endless, boundless universe and who can overturn the decree of fate
Gods	False deities worshipped by nonbelievers and pagans	Celestial beings who live above ground or in the skies, fight demons, and have consumed the elixir of immortality
Heaven	Kingdom of God and final destination of saved souls	Resplendent realms that exist above the earth and are inhabited by sages and gods; temporary abode of those who have accumulated good karma
Sin	Transgression of divine law	Actions with unfavorable reactions

TABLE 18. WORDS OF INDIAN ORIGIN THAT HAVE NO JUDEO-CHRISTIAN-ISLAMIC EQUIVALENTS

Term	Meaning
Kaivalya	State of liberation; omniscience; freedom from the material cycle of birth and death
Karma	Actions whose consequences one is obliged to experience in this life or the next; good or bad karma is usually the function of hindsight, depending on whether the reaction is perceived to be favorable or unfavorable
Lokas	Realms above the feet that are bathed in light
Moksha	Liberation from samsara; entry into kaivalya
Naraka	Subterranean realm ruled by Yama, the king of the dead, where those who have accumulated bad karma suffer after death
Punya	Good karma or karma that results in favorable consequences
Patala	Realms below the feet that are devoid of light; abode of demons and serpents
Paap	Bad karma or karma that results in unfavorable consequences
Rishis	Beings who know the Vedic lore and hence the secrets of the cosmos
Samsara	The world of mind and matter based on karma that is constantly transforming; the tangible, phenomenal world perceived by the senses; the cycle of rebirths
Swarga	Celestial realm of the devas where the best parts of the material world reside
Yoga	Means to liberation; mental control

THE IDEA OF GOD

Let us consider the two words *God* and *gods*. One begins with a capital letter, is singular, and projects the idea of an omnipotent, omnipresent, omniscient singular entity that is the object of reverence in monotheistic religions. The other begins with a lower-case letter, is plural, and connotes deities deemed false by the monotheists. Yahweh is God. Allah is God. But Zeus of the Greeks, Jupiter of the Romans, Horus of the Egyptians, Odin of the Vikings, and Indra of the Aryans are gods—personified natural forces feared by pagans, allegories for emotions conceived by poets, and products of the imagination invented by priests.

Hindus have Gods and gods; there are even Goddesses and goddesses. Depending on one's point of view, Hinduism can be:

- Monotheistic, with belief in one god who is God
- Polytheistic, with belief in many gods of varying power who may or may not be different manifestations of God
- Pantheistic, with belief that God is everything and everything is God
- Pantheistic, with belief that God penetrates every aspect of nature but is nevertheless distinct from it
- Animistic, with belief that everything in the plant, animal, and mineral worlds has its own divine spirit
- Agnostic, with belief that understanding of God can never be empirical
- Henotheistic, with belief in a god or a particular manifestation of God while accepting the validity of other gods or other manifestations of God
- Deistic, with belief that God exists and creates the world but does not participate in daily affairs
- Theistic, with belief that God exists

Divine Principle—Divine Form

Traditionally, Hindus explain their idea of God and Goddess thus: Divinity cannot be contained by definitions, descriptions, and attributes. This impersonal divine principle is known as Brahman in the Upanishads, Purusha in yoga, and Shiva in Tantra. For centuries, the wise have visualized this divine principle as a personality with a name and a form. The name and form, however, are not products of human imagination; they are names and forms revealed by the divine principle itself.

The Divine can be male or female in form. The female form, the Goddess, is known as Maya, Prakriti, or Shakti and represents all things material. In Hinduism *material* means "that which transforms with time" and includes mental processes such as thoughts and feelings. The male form, God, represents all things *spiritual,* or "that which remains constant with time." The male form is visualized as Brahma, Vishnu, and Shiva, who create, sustain, and destroy (see Fig. 1.14). The female form is also visualized as Saraswati, Lakshmi, and Durga, who embody knowledge, wealth, and power. The male forms are active: They perform actions. The female forms are passive: Actions are done to them.

Brahma creates the paradigm we experience as life in order to help us discover our true identities. Vishnu helps us establish perfection in life so that we have a sense of harmony, rhythm, and order. Shiva makes it possible for us to challenge the paradigm, withdraw from it, understand it, control it, and eventually discover our true identities beyond it.

Although there are stories of how Gods and Goddesses come into being, these stories are often sectarian. For example, in Vaishanva manuscripts there are tales of how Brahma and Shiva owe their origin to Vishnu, while in Shakta manuscripts the Goddess is the mother of the male trinity. In Shaiva scriptures the male trinity emerges from Shiva's right half and the female trinity emerges from Shiva's left half. For believers the patron God or

Goddess is *svayambhu,* or self-created and causeless. They seek no explanation for his or her existence. He or she just is.

Since God is self-created and causeless, unlike the rest of the cosmos, natural rock formations are usually worshipped as manifestations of the Divine. One such rock formation is located in the Amarnath caves in the Himalayas (see Fig.1.15), and it is believed to be the symbol of Shiva. In recent times there has been a tendency to place masks with anthropomorphic form on top of these rock formations to make them more comprehensible and accessible to devotees.

Children of the Creator

The gods and goddesses are distinguished from Gods and Goddesses as being the children or grandchildren of the creator, Brahma. They are some of the multitudes of beings engendered by either Brahma or by his mind-born sons known as rishis. Thus gods have parents. This makes them *jiva,* or living beings enmeshed in the matrix of existence and subject to the law of karma, just like humans and even demons.

Scholars generally accept that the word *god* is used in Hinduism to refer to *deva* or *devata,* divinities attributed to Vedic scriptures who after the influence of later theism were reduced to godlings and demigods. Gods and Goddesses emerged following the amalgamation of Vedic thought with tantric thought, which overwhelmed the tide of theism in the post-Vedic era. Temples are built for Gods and Goddesses, not for gods and goddesses. In fact, the word *god* is clearly a mistranslation; early European translators realized that the word *deva* had the same root as the Latin word for God, *Deus.* But they failed to notice that while both Gods and gods were referred to as deva, only Gods were given the epithets *Bhagavan* or *Ishwar,* meaning the embodiment of the supreme divine principle.

The genealogy of any jiva is rather complex and there are different versions in different scriptures. Generally, Brahma, the first manifestation of God whose arrival marks the start of a new kalpa, creates the first woman, Shatarupa. She marries the rishi Daksha. Together they produce women who marry the other mind-born sons of Brahma. These rishis in turn produce the various jivas who populate the cosmos—including gods, goddesses, demons, humans, nymphs, fairies, gnomes, gremlins, goblins, trolls, dwarves, giants, and pixies. Brahma and the primal rishis are therefore given the title *Prajapati,* lord of progeny (see Table 19).

A jiva—whether a god, demon, serpent, or troll—is a living being enmeshed in the cycle of birth and rebirth and who, like humans, yearns for liberation. God, on the other hand, is not bound to the cycle of birth and rebirth. He or she participates in the cycle of his or her own free will, as an expression of divine grace. The differences among gods, demons, and humans are often related to their life span:

- Humans can live up to a hundred years, after which they die and move to the land of the dead awaiting rebirth.
- One human lifetime is equal to one blink of an eye for a god, such as Indra.
- One god's lifetime is equal to one blink of an eye for a God, such as Shiva or Vishnu.
- A god lives as long as the universe survives (one kalpa), because he has consumed the elixir of immortality; however, he does not survive pralaya.
- Serpents can renew their youth because they have rolled on grass stained by the elixir of immortality.
- A demon can die, but can also be resurrected because he possesses the secret of reviving the dead.

Human beings can become gods through righteous conduct, through austerity, by performing the necessary rituals, and by

TABLE 19. JIVAS THAT POPULATE THE HINDU COSMOS

Category	Commonly Used Synonyms	Meaning	Common Characters in Narratives
Apsara	Nymph	Damsel who lives in rivers, entertains gods, and seduces sages	Menaka, Rambha, Urvashi, Ganga
Asura	Demon	Being who lives underground, possesses the power of rejuvenation, and pulls the earth's resources in	Hayagriva, Hiranayaksha, Hiranakashipu, Prahalada, Bali, Virochana, Taraka, Andhaka, Mahisha
Deva or devata	God	Being who lives on the ground or in the skies and pulls the earth's resources out	Indra, Agni, Vayu, Surya, Chandra
Gana	Gnome, troll	Wild and feared wood spirit	Nandi, Bhringi, Vyaghrapada
Gandharva	Fairy	Associated with flowers and fragrance; musician of the gods	Chitraratha
Kinnara, kimpurusha	Centaur, pixie, sphinx	Mysterious earth spirit sometimes associated with music	Tumburu
Manava	Human	Follower of the Vedic code of conduct	Manu, Rama, Krishna, Balarama, Prithu
Naga	Serpent	Keeper of fertility	Vasuki, Karkotaka, Takshaka
Pisacha, vetala, bhuta, preta	Ghosts, vampires	Deceased who have not received proper funerary rites	

TABLE 19. JIVAS THAT POPULATE THE HINDU COSMOS (CONTINUED)

Category	Commonly Used Synonyms	Meaning	Common Characters in Narratives
Pitr	Ancestors, forefathers	Manavas in the land of the dead awaiting rebirth	
Rakshasa	Barbarian, giant	Being who follows the law of the jungle	Ravana, Kumbhakarna, Vibhishanaf
Rishi	Sage or seer	Being who knows the secrets of Vedic lore	Kashyapa, Brihaspati, Shukra, Vasistha, Vishwamitra, Agastya, Durvasa, Bhrigu, Kapila, Kardama
Vanara	Monkey	Tribes whose totem is a monkey	Hanuman, Sugriva
Yaksha	Leprechaun, dwarf	Guardian of treasures	Kubera, Manibhadra

accumulating good karma. Gods and sages can become humans when they stray from the path of righteous conduct. The law of karma applies to demons too, since they are also children of Brahma. The following story demonstrates how a human can become a god by being righteous and upholding dharma against all odds.

∽ Harishchandra ∽
(Bhagavata Purana)

Harishchandra was a righteous king good enough to be a god. To test him rishi Vishwamitra put in his path a series of challenges. Vishwamitra tricked the king into giving up control of his kingdom. When rendered destitute the righteous king left his palace with his wife, Taramati, and son, Rohita. Just as Harishchandra was about to leave the city, Vishwamitra stopped him and said, "You gave me rights over your city. But what about the ritual gift you are obliged to give a rishi for accepting your offering? A king of your status must give at least a thousand gold coins. Failure to do so will demonstrate to the world that you do not respect dharma." Determined to uphold the law of righteous conduct, the penniless Harishchandra sold himself, his wife, and his son on the slave market and gave the sage the gold coins.

Harischandra was thus reduced to the position of a *chandala*, keeper of crematoriums, the lowest rank in the Hindu caste hierarchy. His wife became a maid and a concubine of a priest. Vishwamitra was still not convinced that Harishchandra was meritorious enough to be a god, so he subjected the former king to another test; he caused Harishchandra's son to die of a snakebite. When Taramati brought the corpse to the crematorium, Harishchandra wept but he refused to cremate the child until the fee had been paid. His wife had no money. "Then give me the clothes you wear. Otherwise our child will not be cremated." Taramati, though shocked by his adherence to the rules, obeyed. As she began disrobing, all the gods and sages of the cosmos appeared in the crematorium, amazed by this display of absolute adherence to dharma. They decreed that Harishchandra was fit to be a god.

The following story explains how a misdeed can make "mortals" of "immortals."

༄ The Past Life of Yashoda and Nanda ༄
(Padma Purana)

The rishi Kashyapa and his wife, Aditi, mother of the gods, wanted to perform a yagna. But they could not find a cow to participate in the ritual. The auspicious hour was approaching. Desperate, they stole the cow belonging to the sage Vasistha. For this act they were cursed to be born on earth in the community of cowherds, doomed to face mortality and the pain of having their child taken away from them because he did not actually belong to them.

So it came to pass that Kashyapa and Aditi were reborn as Nanda and Yashoda, a cowherd chieftain and his wife. They raised Krishna, the human incarnation of Vishnu, as their own son. Years later the truth of Krishna's origin was revealed; he was the son of a Yadava chieftain called Vasudeva and his wife, Devaki. To protect the baby from his murderous maternal uncle Kansa, Krishna had been brought to the village of cowherds soon after his birth and swapped with Yashoda's newborn baby girl while the whole village was asleep. When they learned of his true origins, Nanda and Yashoda had no choice but to let Krishna go to his real parents. The parting broke their hearts, just as the loss of the cow broke Vasistha's heart.

Sometimes, even a deed done in accordance with dharma can generate ill will, thereby having a negative consequence. In the following story demons turn out to have been gods in their past lives, and victims of circumstance. Their death at the hands of God is an act of liberation, not punishment. One is thus asked to be wary of morally judging villains.

᨞ The Doorkeepers of Vishnu ᨞
(Bhagavata Purana)

Once a group of sages wanted to pay their respects to Vishnu. When the sages arrived at Vaikuntha the doorkeepers Jaya and Vijaya asked them to wait, as Vishnu was resting. The sages were angry at having been stopped and cursed the doorkeepers to be born on earth as asuras.

When Vishnu learned what had transpired he realized his doorkeepers' cursed fate was the result of their doing their duty diligently. He promised to liberate them from their earthly existence. The two doorkeepers were born as two brothers, Hiranayaksha and Hiranakashipu. Hiranayaksha dragged the earth under the sea, forcing Vishnu to take the form of a boar, plunge into the waters, gore him to death, and raise the earth back to the surface. Hiranakashipu tortured his own son, Prahalada, a devotee of Vishnu, forcing Vishnu to manifest as a monstrous man-lion and tear him to shreds. Thus did Vishnu kill the two asuras and enable his doorkeepers to return to their posts in Vaikuntha.

This story clearly demonstrates that the word *demon* in Hindu lore is not quite what it means in the Christian mythosphere. Although Hindu demons oppose gods, the battle between them is not the battle of good and evil. The asuras Hiranayaksha and Hiranakashipu demonstrate *viparita-bhakti,* or reverse devotion. In hating God these villains remember the divine so many times that they attain enough merit to return to their posts in heaven.

While a hero invokes God through his piety, the villain invokes God through his villainy. In the former case God offers grace; in the latter case God displays rage. In either case God appears, and the presence of God grants salvation. Thus both the hero and the villain end up being blessed. Such a worldview transforms even the worst of deeds as an act of devotion. The apparent punishment from God becomes an act of liberation.

To demonstrate that even villains and demons seek the grace of God, devotees often paint on the walls of temples dedicated to Shiva the images of Ravana, the king of rakshasas, the villain of the Ramayana. Ravana had ten heads and twenty hands. To express his devotion for Shiva he made a lute using one of his heads as the gourd of the lute, one of his arms as the neck of the lute, and his nerves as the strings (see Fig. 1.16). He called this lute Rudra-vina, the lute of Shiva, and with it made music to accompany a hymn called Rudra-stotra that he composed in honor of Shiva. Pleased, Shiva gave Ravana a sword that made him invincible in battle.

Devas are associated with the sun, moon, wind, fire, water, and other principles associated with light, warmth, healing, and fertility. Early translators of Hindu myths were delighted to discover that Hindu gods were no different from the Olympian gods of the Greeks. Thus Indra was Zeus, Kama was Cupid, Yama was Hades, Surya was Helios, Vishwakarma was Hephaestus, and Varuna was Poseidon.

However, translating the word *asura* was not as easy as translating *deva* or *devata,* especially since the word in early Vedic texts was used to qualify exalted beings such as Mithra and Varuna, who were viewed as keepers of moral order. Some scholars thought of asuras as Titans, the divine beings who were overpowered by Greek gods in their quest to become masters of the universe. Others saw them as giants who constantly battled Viking gods and threatened the otherwise bright and warm world with darkness and cold. Still others saw them as the Scottish and Irish Fomorians, original inhabitants of the land, who were overpowered by new immigrants. Since asuras opposed the devas, who had been identified as gods, it was easy to refer to the asuras as enemies of the gods and hence demons. This is more a convenient than a correct translation, as Hindus also worship these demons.

In many rituals invocation is offered to devas and asuras. The devas govern the warmer, brighter half of the year, the *Uttarayana*, from the winter solstice to the summer solstice. The asuras control the other, colder and darker half known as *Dakshinayana*. Thus the demons of Hinduism complement the gods. Hindus also believe that life is influenced by nine astral bodies, the nava-graha, of Hindu astrology (see Fig. 1.17). Two asuras (Rahu, who causes eclipses, and Ketu, who manifests as comets) form part of the nine astral bodies. Prayers are offered to remove their baneful gaze. The nava-graha also include five gods (Sun, Moon, Mars, Mercury, Saturn) and two rishis, one of whom is the guru of the gods (Jupiter) and the other of whom is guru of the demons (Venus).

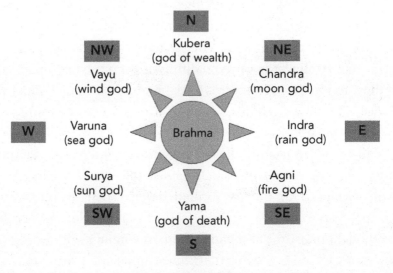

The Guardians of Space

The guardians of space are not all gods either. The guardian of the northern direction is Kubera, the king of yakshas, characters reminiscent of the dwarves and gnomes of pre-Christian European mythology. Above is a diagram indicating the eight guardians of space. A careful study shows that each guardian balances the qualities of the guardian opposite him. Thus Indra, the guardian of east who is associated with rain and fresh water, balances Varuna, the guardian of the west who is associated with the sea and salt water. The wind god Vayu, guardian of the northwest, balances the fire god Agni, guardian of the southeast. The sun god Surya, guardian of the southwest, balances the moon god Chandra, guardian of the north-east. The guardian of the north, Kubera, is associated with fertility and life while the guardian of the south, Yama, lord of the dead, is associated with death.

Hindus worship or propitiate animals, plants, and minerals too, sometimes because they help or harm and sometimes because they represent either God or Goddess. Cows are worshipped because they give milk that serves as food and dung that serves as fuel. Serpents are worshipped because they are associated with fertility and renewal. Both cows and serpents are considered to be animal manifestations of the Goddess. The gander, eagle, and bull, who seem unbound and aloof, are considered animal manifestations of God. The fragrant tulsi shrub is considered the plant manifestation of the Goddess, while the banyan and pipal trees, associated with long life and permanence, are considered the plant manifestations of God. Rivers are worshipped as goddesses—sometimes demure, sometimes violent—because they symbolize the ever-changing nature of life, cleanse the body, and bring life wherever they go. Mountains, on the other hand, are worshipped as gods because they seem rooted, symbolize permanence, block the wandering rain-bearing clouds, and are often the source (father) of rivers (see Table 20).

Every village in India is associated with a robust guardian figure known as the *kshetra-pala* or *vira*. He is depicted rather demonically, with large bloodshot eyes, fangs, and an appetite for blood and entrails. The village itself is personified as the goddess Grama-devi, who nurtures the villagers. Each year her energy is replenished through blood sacrifices; otherwise she turns into a terrifying being who causes drought and unleashes epidemics. The kshetra-pala and Grama-devi are considered the parochial

TABLE 20. SYMBOLS OF GOD AND GODDESS

	God	Goddess
ANIMAL	Gander, eagle, bull	Cow, serpent
GEOMETRIC	Square, upward-pointing triangle	Circle, downward-pointing triangle
MINERAL	Mountains	Rivers
PLANT	Banyan tree, pipal tree	Tulsi shrub

manifestations of God and Goddess. He is identified with either Shiva or Vishnu; she is identified with Kali or Lakshmi. He protects; she provides.

Likewise there are deities only for particular communities, clans, and families. Artisans worship Vishwarkarma, the craftsman of the gods. Merchants worship Kubera, the treasurer of the gods. Accountants worship Chitragupta, the accountant of Yama, the god of death, who keeps a strict account of merits and demerits in his books.

One village goddess, Tuljapur Bhavani (see Fig.1.18), is a parochial manifestation of the Goddess worshipped in Tuljapur, a small village in the western state of Maharashtra. She is also the clan goddess of the martial Maratha community and was patronized by their king, Shivaji. The local tradition holds that Tuljapur Bhavani appeared in Shivaji's dream and gave him a sword to overthrow the Muslim rulers of the land. Hindus who do not live in Maharashtra may not know her, but they will understand her sacredness.

Thus Hindus have not just God but a hierarchy of divinities:

- Personal god
- Family god

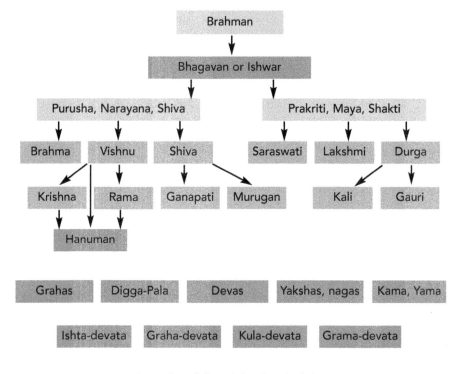

Hierarchy of the Divine in Hinduism

- Household god
- Village god
- Nature spirits
- Gods of life-giving and life-taking processes
- Gods of space and time
- Goddess embodying matter (knowledge, bounty, power) and God embodying spirit (creation, sustenance, destruction)
- Personal godhead
- Impersonal divine principle

The choice of gods worshipped depends on many factors, such as tradition, the religious order to which a person belongs, and the person's attitude toward life. There is no standard theistic practice that can be deemed Hindu. There is no god common to all Hindus. Attempts to find a common concept of God are usually the result of the modern need to align Hinduism with the requirements of an increasingly monotheistic world order.

The object of veneration, whether a family god or an embodiment of the supreme divine principle, is enshrined in a temple. Temples are located everywhere in India: in houses, in business establishments, in fields, in forests, by the wayside, beside rivers, and atop hills. The most magnificent of these shrines are the grand temple complexes of stone, such as those in Puri in Orissa, and Tanjore in Tamil Nadu, built between the tenth and fifteenth centuries of the common era.

A Hindu temple is not a communal prayer hall or the space where the faithful gather and distinguish themselves from the faithless, like a synagogue, church, or mosque. Big or small, the temple is the residence of a god or goddess. The patron deity of a temple is often just a rock with a mask on it or an elaborately decorated idol of stone or metal. An idol has no special value until it is consecrated through a number of elaborate rituals. Devotees throng to temples to have a *darshan,* or glimpse, of this tangible manifestation of the divine. During darshan, the devotees absorb the grace of the deity and take it with them in their secular lives. With constant exposure, the power of the idol gradually wanes until it is restored through rituals. To minimize the loss of aura, the deity is isolated in a special room called *garbha griha,* or the womb room, which is rather dark, cramped, and off limits to the public. Only priests who have been ritually cleansed are allowed to enter the room and touch the idol. However, once a year, for the benefit of devotees the idol is taken out of the room and into the streets in a grand procession.

To retain the sacred power of the presiding deity and to keep out invading armies, high walls enclose the Hindu temple. The gateways, especially in the south, are huge, covered with images from myths and legends so as to scare away demons, glorify the resident god, and demonstrate the wealth and power of the temple's builder (see Fig. 1.19). Around the main shrine are smaller shrines of other gods and goddesses. There are also communal kitchens, marriage halls, dance halls, and houses for hundreds of priests. The temple itself is viewed as a celestial chariot, is usually built on a platform, and is occasionally shaped like a turtle or lotus. The garbha griha lies at its heart. Its roof is pyramidal in South Indian temples (Dravida style) and curvilinear in North Indian temples (Nagara style). A sacred pot is placed and a flag hoisted atop this roof. Around the central shrine is a vestibule through which devotees can circumambulate the shrine to express their devotion. In front is a hall of pillars where devotees gather before God.

Within the temple, darshan is allowed only during special periods of the day and only for a brief period of time. During darshan devotees express their adoration, make offerings, present petitions, and seek divine blessing. Later devotees collect the remains of all ritual offerings (food, water, sandal paste, flowers, clothes), as these are considered to transmit divine grace. Even the heat of the lamp that is waved before the idol is sought by all, as it is considered a medium of the deity's aura.

Scenes from myths and epics are often carved on temple walls. There are images of animals, plants, gods, demons, sages, courtesans, priests, and warriors. Sex and violence are graphically depicted. An attempt is thus made to capture all that radiates out of the divine located at the heart of the shrine. Thus the Hindu temple is an architectural expression of Hindu metaphysics.

Temple wall art depicts all that exists in the cosmos, even those beings and events that challenge the limits of human imagination. Each carving, however carnal, violent, and fantastic, is perceived as a form of God. In the detail depicted in Fig. 1.20, God is presented as a householder with his consort, as a terrifying demon holding many weapons in his many arms, and as a multiheaded god who serenely witnesses the conundrums of life with a mysterious smile on his many faces.

DEVILS AND DEMONS

None of the pre-Christian mythologies of Europe gave importance to the idea of an all-powerful God. Their mythosphere was inhabited by myriad beings, including those we today refer to as gods, demons, and humans. The Norse had Aesir, Vanir, dwarves, elves, giants, nymphs, and trolls. The Greeks had Olympians; Titans; giants; satyrs; fauns; and nymphs known as oreads, dryads, and Nereids who lived in caves, trees, and rivers. The Celts had fairies, gnomes, pixies, gremlins, leprechauns, and goblins. All these are reminiscent of the asuras, gandharvas, apsaras, kinnaras, kimpurushas, vidyadharas, yakshas, nagas, rakshasas, and vanaras found in the Hindu mythosphere.

Yakshas, for example, are potbellied forest spirits who love riddles and guard treasures (see Fig. 1.21). Their city, Alakapuri, is located in the north. Their king, Kubera, is the treasurer of the gods. He has a pet golden mongoose that spits out gems. Humans pull Kubera's chariot. A miser, Kubera realized money could not buy everything when he lost an eye and had to replace it with a prosthetic eye made of gold. In the Indian mythosphere, each type of spirit is similarly defined by its own particular set of attributes.

The characters populating ancient mythospheres can be broadly divided into those who are harmful to humankind and those who are helpful. But this division is not simple. A yaksha could help or harm. A nymph could enchant or enlighten. A god could kill to liberate a demon or to punish a human. Every event in life, good or bad, a great harvest or a terrible storm, results from the complex interaction between these creatures.

A clearly defined God or Satan was not always in existence. Jupiter, though king of the gods, is hardly Yahweh. Loki, the trickster of Nordic tradition, though a mischief-monger and gatecrasher who ultimately though unwittingly heralds the death of the gods, cannot be equated with Satan. The Fomors of Ireland were feared and fought, but were never quite visualized as demons. Neither the Greek Cronus, who is overpowered by Zeus, nor the Mesopotamian Tiamat, who is overpowered by the god Madruk, qualifies as evil. Yet modern retellings of these ancient myths demonstrate a need to qualify all battles as the battle of good over evil. Thus the Disney animation film *Hercules* depicts Hades, god of the underworld, demonically. Even Tolkien's *Lord of the Rings,* which is based on Nordic mythology, refers to an all-consuming evil force that needs to be overpowered by the heroes. This is clearly mythopoesis in a world dominated by the Manichaean ideology that views every conflict as the battle between good and evil.

Interestingly, the earliest Judaic scriptures are not concerned with the idea of evil: Bad things happened when Yahweh was disobeyed, ignored, or sidelined by false gods. The idea of evil is believed to have entered Judaism, Christianity, and Islam from the Zoroastrian narratives of ancient Persia. These tales speak of life on earth as an eternal struggle between the good Ahura Mazda and the bad Angra Manyu. These ideas were popular in Babylon during the days of exile following the destruction of Solomon's temple in Jerusalem. Zoroaster was the Persian prophet who educated his people on how to overpower Angra Manyu's evil in their daily lives.

The word *evil* is used in Zoroastrian, Judaic, Christian, and Islamic paradigms to explain events that cannot be attributed to the divine. For the followers of Zoroaster, death, disease, smoke, poverty, and pain were the creations of the evil one who polluted the perfect creation of the Ahura Mazda, the supreme god. In the Bible, imperfection is the result of Adam and Eve succumbing to the temptations of the serpent, who is later identified as the devil, a jealous and fallen angel.

Not all cultures needed the idea of evil to explain the undesirable. In pre-Christian Europe, bad things happened because of unfriendly wood spirits or jealous gods. In ancient Mesopotamia, the gods made humans mortal in order to make servants of them. All calamities were divine whips used to ensure the obedience of man.

In Hinduism the law of karma explains bad happenings. According to this law every event is a reaction to the past. Good things happen because of merits earned by good deeds, or *punya*. Bad things happen because of demerits earned by bad deeds, or *paap*. There is no place for evil. Hence no Indian language has a synonym for the word.

Hindu narratives constantly offer explanations for any event. Nothing happens spontaneously. Good things happen because of boons; bad things happen because of a curse. Boons and curses served as narrative tools to explain the idea of karma. Boons and curses help answer the why of uncomfortable experiences.

∽ Why Rama Went into Exile ∽
(Ramayana)

Dasharatha's favorite wife Kaikeyi had saved his life in battle. In gratitude he had promised to fulfill three of her wishes. On the eve of her stepson Rama's coronation she asked for the three wishes: "Let Rama renounce the throne, let him live in the forest as a hermit for fourteen years, let my son Bharata rule in his place." Dasharatha had no choice but to fulfill her wishes.

When Rama left the city Dasharatha died of a broken heart. This tragedy was attributed to an unfortunate event that had occurred when the king was young. During a hunting trip he had accidentally shot a young man called Shravana, the only child and caretaker of a blind couple. As they mourned the death of their son, the couple cursed Dasharatha that he would die of a broken heart following separation from his son.

The following story explains why Krishna had to die a terrible death, even though he was responsible for bringing order on earth. A good deed need not result in a good fate, for a good deed may not be good for everyone.

⤫ The Curse of Gandhari ⤬
(Mahabharata)

With the help of Krishna, the Pandavas killed their cousins the Kauravas and established righteousness in the land. Gandhari, the mother of the Kauravas, was inconsolable in her grief. She cursed Krishna that he would witness the death of his children and kinsmen, after which he would suffer an ignominious death at the hands of a common hunter.

Actions that reap favorable reactions are known as *punya;* those that reap unfavorable actions are known as *paap.* Curses are the result of paap, while boons are the result of punya. Although the word *paap* is commonly translated as sin, its antonym *punya* has no synonym in English. In the biblical mythosphere, one either sins or does not sin. The concept of merit and demerit does not fit in with ease. While acts of kindness and devotion can determine one's fate in the final afterlife on the day of judgment, they certainly do not influence future *lives.*

At a more subtle level an action is deemed to be paap or punya in hindsight. When good things happen, we say that our past deeds were good. Likewise, when bad things happen, we say that our past deeds were bad. When the action is performed, we are quite oblivious of its implications.

In the following story a hunter does a good deed without meaning to but obtains the merits nevertheless.

⤫ The Offering of Bel Leaves ⤬
(Linga Purana)

A hunter got lost in the forest and took refuge on top of a tree to protect himself from wild animals during the night. The tree happened to be the bel tree, which was much loved by Shiva. The branches of the tree shook as the hunter climbed to the top, causing leaves to fall on a linga, or phallus, below. Thus the hunter inadvertently made offerings to Shiva, pleasing the god who then granted the hunter freedom from the cycle of rebirths.

Whether an event is good or bad depends entirely on one's perspective. For example, in the Ramayana the exile of Rama into the forest is an unhappy event. But it pleases the gods as it sets the stage for the confrontation between Rama and Ravana and the latter's ultimate defeat.

In the absence of evil there is no need for Satan in the Hindu mythosphere. However, there are a whole host of villains in epics and scriptures. These are villains who can be classified in three distinct categories:

1. Asuras who fight gods
2. Rakshasas who fight humans
3. Pisachas who fight ancestors

Since devas are considered gods, asuras—the gods' eternal enemies—are considered demons. But these demons are in no way morally inferior to the gods. In fact, in many cases they are superior. Asura kings such as Prahalada, Virochana, and Bali are associated with virtues such as devotion, justice, and generosity.

According to the Vamana Purana, Bali led the asuras, defeated all the gods, and became master of the three worlds. He was loved by all because of his generosity. The gods, impoverished in defeat, approached Vishnu for help. He said, "Bali's generosity will be his undoing." Vishnu approached Bali in the form of a dwarf and asked as an offering three paces of land. Bali agreed without a moment's hesitation. The dwarf instantly turned into a giant. With two paces he covered the sky and the atmosphere.

With the third he shoved Bali to the subterranean regions where all asuras belong (see Fig. 1.22).

In narratives devas are depicted as devious, cunning, treacherous, and sometimes even immoral, constantly seeking the embraces of wives in the absence of their husbands.

∽ Indra Seduces Ahalya ∽
(Ramayana)

While the sage Gautama was away, Indra seduced Gautama's wife, Ahalya. As they made love the sage returned. Enraged, he turned his wife into stone. He castrated Indra and caused his body to be covered with a thousand vaginas.

This story clearly suggests that to reduce the battle of devas and asuras into the battle of gods and demons or the battle between good and evil is more convenient than convincing. The battle of devas and asuras is a recurring theme in the Hindu mythosphere captured in the diagram on the next page. Typically it begins with the demons acquiring a boon that allows them to overpower the gods. It ends with a God or Goddess enabling the gods to outfox the demon. In the earliest versions of this battle, there is no intervention of God or Goddess. The participation of the latter began when theistic principles overwhelmed the earlier ritualistic Vedic traditions.

Various theistic schools employ the theme of the cosmic battle to establish the supremacy of their respective patron deities. For example, tales from the holy books of the Vaishnavas inform devotees how Vishnu—preserver of cosmic order—incarnates himself in various forms to overpower demons. According to the Shaivas, when Vishnu fails to defeat the asuras Shiva has to be roused from his meditation. According to Shaktas, who cite tales from the Devi Bhagvata Purana, when Shiva fails too, the Goddess comes to the rescue.

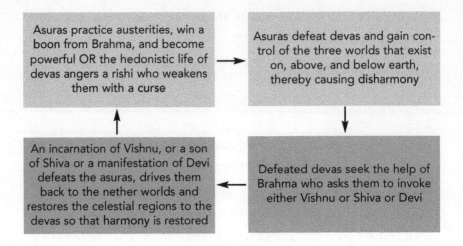

Cycle of Victories and Defeats Involving the Gods and Demons

According to the Devi Bhagavata Purana of the Shaktas, Mahisha, the asura king, obtained from Brahma a boon by virtue of which no plant, animal, human, demon, or god could kill him. Thus empowered, Mahisha drove the devas out of the celestial regions. They went to their father, Brahma, who directed them to Vishnu, who directed them to Shiva. Shiva advised them to release their powers, which emerged from all their mouths in the form of fire. The fires fused and out of it emerged a magnificent warrior woman called Durga with eight arms. She rode a lion, attacked Mahisha and other asuras, and impaled them with her trident (see Fig. 1.23). She succeeded because Mahisha had not bothered to seek protection from women.

The peace that follows the defeat of an asura is only a temporary reprieve until a new demon appears and repeats the cycle of war and victory. War is a reaction to peace and vice versa. There is something rhythmic in the shifting fortunes of the devas and asuras. Neither is defeated permanently; both are equally matched. This suggests that the existence of asuras is somehow necessary for the world. Without them there is imbalance. When God manifests he does not destroy the asura, he merely pushes him to the nether regions where he belongs (see Table 21).

The antagonism of devas and asuras is necessary for the cosmos. This idea is driven home by the following narrative, in which Shri, the goddess of wealth and fortune, can only be churned out of the ocean when both asuras and devas participate (see Fig. 1.24).

✃ Churning the Ocean to Find Shri ✃ (Bhagavata Purana)

Shri once disappeared from the earth. The world was thus barren and bereft of joy. The devas went to Vishnu, who said that since Shri had dissolved herself into the ocean of milk she had to be churned out. This could not be done without the help of the

TABLE 21. COMPLEMENTARY ANTAGONISTS IN THE HINDU MYTHOSPHERE

Devas	Asuras
Brihaspati, lord of Jupiter, is their guru	Shukra, lord of Venus, is their guru
Children of Aditi by Prajpati Kashyapa	Children of Diti and Danu by Prajapati Kashyapa
Drink elixir of immortality	Possess secret of resurrecting the dead
Live aboveground and in skies	Live underground
Powerful from winter solstice to summer solstice	Powerful from summer solstice to winter solstice
Victory enables them to live in radiant celestial regions and enjoy material and sensual delights	Defeat pushes them back into the dark and gloomy subterranean realms where they live in cities of gold

asuras. The asuras missed Shri too. So they forgot their differences with the devas and came together to churn the ocean.
Under Vishnu's instruction, the bird king Garuda carried Meru,
the mountain king, to the center of the ocean to serve as the
spindle of the churn. Akupara, the turtle king, prevented the
mountain from sinking. Vasuki, the serpent king, wound himself
round the mountain. The devas caught his tail end, the asuras
grabbed his neck, and the churning began. The ocean frothed
and fumed for aeons until finally the waters coagulated to reveal
fabulous treasures, the most delightful of which was Shri. There
emerged from the ocean a pot of *amrita*, the elixir of immortality. Both the devas and asuras fought over it. Vishnu took the
form of Mohini, the enchantress. She offered to divide the drink
equally, but while the asuras were entranced by her beguiling
smile she poured the drink down the throats of devas. Thus
empowered, the devas defeated the asuras and claimed the
treasures of the ocean for themselves.

The devas and the asuras serve as the force and counterforce
of the churn. But Vishnu ensures that all the treasures that
emerge, including Shri, ultimately end up in the hands of the
devas. Thus the abode of the gods is associated with the best of
animal, plant, and mineral wealth:

- Kamadhenu, the desire-manifesting cow
- Kalpataru, the wish-fulfilling tree
- Parasmani, the dream-realizing gem

When asuras overpower the devas they take control of this
wealth. When devas defeat the asuras this wealth is released. It is
said that even the queen of the gods, Indra's wife, Pulomi, is the
daughter of the asura Puloman, indicating that all the wonders of
the realm of the gods emerge from the realm of the demons.

Asuras are thus not evil creatures but sons of Brahma who drag the wealth of the cosmos to their subterranean realms. The sun god, moon god, rain god, fire god, and wind god release this wealth by pulling our plants, striking our water, and melting our rocks for minerals.

The actions of devas benefit humans. Hence for humans, devas are "gods" and asuras are "demons." Helpful devas are worthy of adoration, reverence, offerings, and empowering rituals. The asuras may be necessary for the process of life, but undesirable for livelihood.

Nagas, or serpent gods, live underground and are associated with the powers of fertility and renewal (see Fig. 1.25). There are many narratives describing the conflict between serpents and eagles. The underlying theme seems to be the same as in the conflict between the asuras and devas. The earthbound naga drags the wealth of the earth downward while the skybound garuda pulls the wealth of the earth upward. Unlike asuras, nagas are worshipped. The epic Rajatarangini of Kalhana informs us that when the king of Kashmir refused to worship nagas his kingdom suffered a great drought. In Vishnu temples, the king of eagles, who serves as Vishnu's mount, is shown holding a serpent with its beak and claws, suggesting the control of culture over nature's slippery fertility.

In the Ramayana, another type of jiva, the rakshasas, are described as violent beings who disturb the meditation and rituals of rishis. As with asuras, rakshasas are not considered evil either, but their actions are not favorable to humans. Tadaka, Khara, and Dushana disturb Vishwamitra so much that he is forced to seek the protection of Dasharatha and his sons. Rakshasas are also carnal beings who do not respect marriage. Their king, Ravana, abducts the wife of Sita, determined to make her his queen. Ravana's sister tries to marry Rama by force, even when he says that he is faithful to his wife. All this suggests that the rakshasas follow the law of the jungle, where sex and violence are unrestrained and might is right. Rama, on the other hand, is a faithful husband and a conscientious warrior; his sexual and violent urges are in control. He follows dharma, the Vedic code of civilized conduct.

The battle between Rama and Ravana is not about good and evil but about culture and nature. In Rama's world the weak are protected by the strong. In Ravana's world there is no room for the weak. Rama does his duty even if it means sacrificing personal happiness. He gives up his kingdom on his father's orders without remorse or resentment and makes way for his brother Bharata. Ravana, on the other hand, does what pleases him. He drives his brother Kubera out of Lanka and lays claim to the crown.

Pitrs are forefathers that are in the land of the dead awaiting rebirth. Their descendents in the land of the living remember them, feed them, and make promises to facilitate their rebirth by producing children through funerary rituals known as *shraadh*. Some pitrs have no descendents in the land of the living, or nobody remembers them. Nobody performs funerary rituals in their honor. They are hungry, restless, and often without hope of ever being reborn. Anxious and angry, they turn into ghosts, ghouls, and vampires and trouble both the living and the dead, demanding attention and appeasement. Unlike the ghosts and vampires of Christian mythology, they don't need to be exorcised and driven away. They need to calmed and reassured through peace-bestowing *atma-shanti* rituals (see Table 22).

CREATION WITH A DIFFERENCE

In the Bible no explanation is given for how Yahweh comes into being. He is simply the beginning and one has to accept that. Yahweh creates the world out of nothingness in seven days before

TABLE 22. EXPLANATIONS FOR THE ETERNAL CONFLICTS IN THE
         COSMOS

Conflict	Explanation
Deva versus asura	Forces of nature competing to pull the wealth of nature's bounty aboveground or underground
Manava versus rakshasa	Struggle between those who follow the code of human civilization based on duties and deference and those who follow the law of the jungle based on might
Naga versus garuda	Competition between earthbound and skybound natural spirits
Pitr versus pisachas	Fight between departed souls whose descendents respect them, offer them food, and give them a chance to be reborn by producing children and departed souls who are forgotten by the living

he rests. He remains distinct from his creation, which is perfect until the first human couple, Adam and Eve, ignore his warning and eat the fruit of knowledge, thus succumbing to the temptations presented by the serpent. Judaic, Christian, and biblical versions of this narrative barely stray from the fundamental idea that an all-powerful creator created a perfect world out of nothingness, and its perfection was marred by human disobedience.

In Hindu scriptures there are many versions of creation, with different plots and protagonists. This reflects the many transformations Hinduism has gone through in the last four thousand years, the many ideas that have been assimilated into and have emerged from it. Often narratives are strategic, attempting to show the greatness of one patron deity over another. The following story reflects how goddess worshippers describe the creation of the world. The story has no scriptural basis but is the theme of many folk songs and folk stories. It is considered the earliest story of creation, belonging to ancient Indian tribes and to matriarchal cultures that existed before the arrival and eventual domination of the patriarchal Vedic culture.

∾ The Birth of the Three Gods ∾
(Folklore)

In the beginning the supreme Goddess Adi Shakti laid three eggs in a lotus. From these three eggs emerged the three worlds and the three gods: Brahma, Vishnu, and Shiva. Desire awoke in the heart of the Goddess, who asked the Gods to make love to her. "But you are our mother," said Brahma and Vishnu, shying away. The Goddess was angry at being rejected and reduced the two Gods to ashes by casting a glance of her fiery third eye. She then turned to Shiva, who agreed to make love to her if she gave him her eye. She did. Shiva used it to reduce her to ashes and revive the other two Gods.

Brahma, Vishnu, and Shiva then decided to populate the world with living beings, but they could not do so without wives. They gathered around the heap of ash that was once Adi Shakti, divided it into three parts, and with the power of the third eye created the three Goddesses Saraswati, Lakshmi, and Gauri. The three Goddesses married the three Gods and together they populated the cosmos with all manner of plants, animals, and other living things, including gods, demons, and humans.

In the classical version of creation, in the beginning the first being becomes aware of itself and wonders what its identity is. The resulting creation is an attempt to unravel this mystery. The earliest version of this narrative is found in the Veda and the Upanishads, which were written before the common era. Later versions with strong theistic leanings were written in the early part of the last millennium. When devotees of Vishnu narrate the story, Vishnu takes center stage. When devotees of Shiva tell the story, Shiva plays a more important role. In the Upanishads the first being is called Purusha; in the Puranas, this being is Brahma.

৩৩ Brahma Opens His Eyes ৩৩
(Vishnu Purana)

In the beginning a lotus bloomed. Within sat Brahma. He opened his eyes and realized he was all alone. Afraid, he sought the origin of the lotus he sat on. It emerged from the navel of Vishnu, who slept on the coils of the serpent Ananta-Sesha on the surface of a boundless ocean of milk. Having been informed by Vishnu, Brahma set about creating living beings.

Although Brahma is called the creator of the world, the narrative clearly indicates that he does not create the physical world out of nothingness; the world preexists him. But no one perceives this world, for even Vishnu is in dreamless sleep—a state in which one is not aware of oneself, much less of the environment. In all practicality, nothing exists. The following lines from the Rig Veda ponder this state: "Who knows what existed then? Even the gods came later."

In Hindu metaphysics an entity comes into being only when one is aware of it. No observation exists independent of the observer. For the cosmos to be created someone must perceive it. Perception holds the spark of creation. In the absence of perception everything is unmanifest.

Just as our lives begin when we wake up, so does the Hindu world begin its life when Brahma opens his eyes. The awakening of Vishnu, the blooming of the lotus from his navel, the appearance of Brahma—all represent the quickening of consciousness from a state of dreamlessness to a state of alertness, from unawareness to awareness. This awakening of consciousness is vital to creation, for then one becomes sensitive to experience. And with this sensitivity time becomes sequential and space comes to possess three dimensions. Energy comes to occupy space and it transforms with time. Awareness lies at the root of the creative process. Brahma, as the first being to be aware, to make manifest the unmanifest, is therefore the creator.

Brahma distinguishes between himself and the rest of the cosmos. He knows what he is not, but he does not know who he is. This lack of knowledge makes him restless, anxious, and fearful. The quest for answers inspires the following story.

∽ Brahma's Mind-Born Sons ∽
(Brahmavaivarta Purana)

When Brahma first opened his eyes he was filled with the fear that comes with the awareness that one exists and that one exists alone. As he was longing for company, he created children: four men molded out of his thoughts. Brahma asked his mind-born sons to multiply, but they refused and disappeared.

The four mind-born beings created asexually are referred to as *Sanat-kumars,* the eternally youthful ones. They are visualized as four prepubescent boys. Their male gender indicates that they are, like Brahma, sensitive to experience. Prepubescence is an indicator that they are innocent of sexual thoughts. Sex presupposes the existence of two beings: oneself and the rest. When Brahma demands that his creations be sexual, he is demanding that they, like him, acknowledge the split. The Sanat-kumars refuse to do so; they don't want to, or perhaps they don't know how. Innocent of the split, they are self-contained and hence eternally youthful.

The story of the Sanat-kumars drives home the importance of yearning in the creative process. Brahma creates because he yearns to know his true identity. Brahma does not give up after the disappearance of his first four mind-born sons. He proceeds to create seven more. These seven creations are not boys but men. They are aware of the split. They are willing to reproduce. But how?

ᘛ Brahma Splits Himself ᘚ
(Shiva Purana)

Brahma's sons were willing to populate the cosmos but did not know how. As Brahma pondered this question he saw a vision of Shiva, and his left half was a woman. Inspired, Brahma split himself in two. From his left half he created woman.

Such was the woman's beauty that desire rose in the heart of Brahma and his sons. Desire took the form of Kandarpa, the winsome god of lust, who rode a parrot and aroused the five senses by shooting his five flower-tipped arrows with his sugarcane bow. Overwhelmed by yearning to embrace this woman, Brahma and his sons spurted semen and began to multiply.

The sexual act is a metaphor for acknowledging the material reality that is perceived as a woman. That the material reality exists within Brahma indicates that creation is a subjective phenomenon, not an objective event. God and Goddess, spiritual and material realities, always exist. But creation happens only when God perceives the Goddess. Goddess exists to help God know himself. She is born of him. He knows himself because of her. Each one needs the other.

In art the Goddess is often shown seated on God's lap, holding a mirror up to his face (see Fig. 1.26). She helps him know who he is. The mirror, a creation of the Goddess and hence a material entity, is the symbol of the intellect. It enables spiritual reality to know itself by distinguishing it from material reality. At a microcosmic level this image informs all individuals to focus on learning from life's experiences. It holds the key to the mystery of life, the answer to that eternal question of all sentient beings: Who am I?

By acknowledging material reality all jivas are drawn into the matrix of existence. Inside samsara, all things change. All that comes into being must cease to be. Brahma, the creator, thus also creates Mrityu, the goddess of death and the embodiment of change.

∾ The Creation of Death ∾
(Mahabharata)

Brahma's children multiplied but did not die. Soon the cosmos was overflowing with jivas, which alarmed Brahma, who created Mrityu, the goddess of death. When informed of her duty Mrityu ran away. She relented only when told that all those she would kill would be reborn. She would kill only the material, and hence mortal, component of a jiva.

Since Brahma creates the first woman she is called his daughter. Her name, Shatarupa, "she of myriad forms," acknowledges that she is the personification of material reality. She is also known as Saraswati, the goddess of knowledge. Interestingly, Saraswati, the daughter of Brahma, is also known as his consort. This is because as the goddess of knowledge, she fulfills Brahma's quest for knowledge. What Brahma begins with ignorance Saraswati ends with enlightenment.

Saraswati embodies the wisdom and inspiration contained in nature. She wears a simple white sari indicative of her spiritual and transcendental nature (see Fig. 1.27). She makes no attempt to allure the observer; she is aloof and serene. The book and lute she holds indicate her association with education and the arts. He who seeks her must come to her. She is difficult to get, but once acquired she is ever faithful. Saraswati is associated with storks, which symbolize concentration, and ganders, which symbolize intellectual discrimination (ganders are believed to possess the power to separate milk from water). She humbles the proud peacock. She is the answer to Brahma's question, Who am I? Because the answer is born of the question, and because question and answers need each other, she is both the daughter and consort of Brahma.

Unfortunately, when Brahma first sees his creation Saraswati, he looks upon her not as the medium of realization but as an object of pleasure. Rather than learning from her, he desires her.

ᴄᴧᴐ Transformations of the Daughter ᴄᴧᴐ (Brihadaranyaka Upanishad)

The daughter took to the skies in the form of a goose to avoid her father's lustful gaze. Brahma chased her in the form of a gander. She then transformed into a cow and then a mare. Brahma kept up the pursuit in the forms of a bull and a horse. Every time the daughter tried to escape by taking the form of an animal or bird, Brahma followed her as the corresponding male. Thus all animals came into being.

In the Puranas the daughter circumambulates Brahma, who so desires her that he sprouts four heads in the four cardinal directions to see her at all times. When she moves to the sky to avoid his gaze, he sprouts a fifth head that voices his carnal intentions, to the horror of his assembled sons.

In the stories from both the Upanishads and the Puranas, the daughter transforms and moves as all material things do. Brahma reacts to this by defining and redefining himself to accommodate her. Each time he comes to possess a new identity. But these identities are false; as reactions to material transformations, they are as ephemeral as the material transformations that inspired them. Brahma's heads thus symbolize the ego, which is nothing but a reaction to experiences and expectations in samsara.

In order to achieve self-realization the false identity imposed by the ego must be crushed. In the Brahmana texts, Shiva as Rudra pierces Brahma with an arrow, preventing the father from mounting the daughter. In the Puranas, Shiva as Bhairava wrenches off Brahma's fifth head. The incestuous desire of the father transforms the path of self-realization into the path of self-gratification.

But the existence of the ego is necessary for self-preservation, self-propagation, and self-actualization. Hence Shiva allows the four heads of Brahma to stay. Shiva appears only when the boundaries are crossed, when interaction with material reality is inspired by the desire to possess and control and when the subject forgets that the object is his own creation that exists to "hold the mirror."

Brahma may have created the paradigm that holds the answer to the eternal question, Who am I? But until the answer is found, the medium of realization seems like the cause of many a conundrum: pleasure and pain, hope and frustration, life and death. Hence the Hindu creator, unlike the creator in the Judeo-Christian-Islamic paradigms, is considered unworthy of worship.

HEAVEN OR HELL

Half of humanity believes that there is only one life followed by either nothingness or an eternal hereafter. The other half believes that each life is followed by another life and that all living beings are trapped in a never-ending cycle of rebirths. In the former ideology the goal is to secure a place in heaven, not hell. In the latter the aim is to find permanence within the ever-changing material world or simply transcend it.

Hindus belong to the latter category. Following death a person can end up in either Pitr-loka, the land of ancestors (also known as Yama-loka), and await rebirth, or Swarga-loka, heaven, where he is released from the cycle of rebirths.

Unfortunately, not everything is so simple. There are many heavens in the Hindu cosmology, which are listed in the table below (see Table 23).

In Indra-loka is a tree that never withers and bears any fruit one wishes for (Kalpataru); a never-aging cow that provides all that one wants (Kamadhenu); a gem that fulfills every wish (paras-mani); a pot that is always full of grain and gold (akshaya-patra); a nectar that keeps the devas healthy, youthful, and immortal (amrita); a goddess (Varuni) who ensures an endless flow of wine; and buxom damsels (the apsaras Rambha, Urvashi, and Menaka), well versed in the sixty-four arts, who sing, dance, and provide eternal entertainment. The devas who live in Indra-loka are forever in a state of pleasure, prosperity, and power. Their city is the very embodiment of affluence and abundance. It is the Hindu paradise. This is where humans end up after accumulating lifetimes

TABLE 23. THE MANY HEAVENS OF HINDUISM

Heaven	Abode of
Brahma-loka	Brahma, the creator
Go-loka	Krishna
Indra-loka (Amravati)	Devas
Satya-loka	Rishis and enlightened beings
Shiva-loka (Kailasa)	Shiva
Vishnu-loka (Vaikuntha)	Vishnu, the sustainer

of good karma by performing the ritual of yagna, by enduring austere tapasya, or by unquestioningly fulfilling the social role (dharma) that is determined by their station in society and stage in life. Entry to Indra-loka is not easy, as the devas do everything in their power to block entry.

⌘ The Birth of Urvashi ⌘
(Bhagavata Purana)

The sages Nara and Narayana were performing tapasya. To tempt them out of their austerities, the gods sent nymphs to seduce them. Rather than succumb to temptations, the two sages slapped their thighs and created a damsel called Urvashi, who ended up seducing the gods. The gods saluted these great sages, who were destined for heavens higher than that of Indra.

Since the residents of Indra-loka drink amrita, they do not die. They live forever, or at least until pralaya, when everything in the cosmos, including the edifice of the heavens, collapses. In the heavens of God—Brahma-loka, Vishnu-loka, Go-loka, and Shiva-loka (graded according to which manifestation of God one believes in)—one is unaffected by pralaya too. With God one witnesses the birth and death of universes, civilizations, gods, demons, and humans.

As Hinduism evolved and moved away from ritualism to theism, as Indra was overshadowed by more powerful Gods, such as Vishnu and Shiva, Indra's heaven waned in significance. It was seen as a place of temporary pleasure, from where one could be cast out. Residents of Indra-loka were not content; desire still lingered in their hearts.

ᖆ Mahabhisha ᖆ
(Mahabharata)

Mahabhisha was allowed to enter Indra-loka, as he had helped the devas defeat the asuras. While Mahabhisha was in Indra-loka the river nymph Ganga paid the gods a visit. As she entered, her upper garment slipped off. The gods lowered their eyes, but Mahabhisha stared without shame. This display of lust angered Indra, who cursed Mahabhisha to return to earth, where Ganga would break his heart.

Unlike Indra-loka, Vishnu-loka and Shiva-loka are heavens for those who have broken free from the cycle of rebirth. The means to break free is *yoga,* which simply put means "mental control." Yoga yokes the mind so that it is not swept away by the current of samsara. Masters of yoga refuse to react with the material world. They renounce society, become ascetics, bridle their senses, suppress their egos, and meditate until they discover their true identities. Since the world is seen as a creation of the mind, mental control is viewed as cosmic control. He who has absolute power over the mind has absolute power over the cosmos. He thus becomes one with God, unfettered by the rules governing material reality. The yoga master could appear and disappear at will, fly in the air, walk on water, and even order the gods around (see Table 24).

Ancestors, however, do not appreciate these mental-control actions, as their passage to the land of the living is blocked by the ascetic's refusal to reproduce. The ancestors appear in dreams and remind ascetics of their biological obligation.

Ꮼ Agastya's Ancestors Ꮼ
(Mahabharata)

Agastya had renounced the world to perform yoga. One night he saw in a dream the plight of his ancestors in Yama-loka. They hung upside down over a bottomless pit. "Father children so that we may be reborn or suffer an eternity in the hell known as Put, which is reserved for childless men," they cried. Agastya therefore fathered a child and returned to his quest for the soul.

The common householder cannot renounce society to discover the self. For the householder seeking release there is bhakti: liberation achieved by abandoning oneself to the grace of God, as Markandeya does in the following story (see Fig. 1.28).

Ꮼ Heaven for Markandeya Ꮼ
(Linga Purana)

Markandeya's parents were childless for a long time. So they invoked Shiva, who offered either a stupid child with a long life

TABLE 24. DIFFERENT TYPES OF YOGA

Type of Yoga	Means for Mental (Cosmic) Control
Bhakti	Humility and devotion
Gyan	Intellectual activity
Hatha	Physical austerities
Karma	Detached participation in worldly affairs
Mantra (Japa)	Hymns and chants
Tantra (Laya)	Rituals

or an intelligent child with a short life. The couple chose the latter and were blessed with Markandeya, a boy destined to die when he was sixteen. On the eve of his sixteenth birthday, Markandeya decided to spend his remaining hours in the land of the living by worshipping Shiva. At the appointed hour Yama appeared. Markandeya, however, had not finished his prayers. He requested that Yama wait for a while. Yama laughed, reminding the boy that death waits for no one. He flung his noose and began dragging out Markandeya's life breath. Markandeya abandoned himself to Shiva with a cry; upon hearing it Shiva appeared, kicked Yama away, and rescued his devotee from death. Markandeya wound up in Kailasa, the abode of Shiva, where he lived forever as a young boy.

How can the soul that has no form reside in heaven? And how can the soul be reborn if it is immortal? To answer these questions Hindu metaphysicians constructed a rather elaborate anatomy. The body was seen as composed of two parts: the undying soul, which is intangible, and the impermanent body, which is tangible. As long as the immortal soul is not realized, rebirth happens. The mortal body possessed three components: the flesh, the mind, and the cache of karmas known as gross, subtle, and causal bodies, respectively.

Death claims the flesh and the mind but not the cache of karma. The causal body survives death. By the law of karma that forms the fundamental principle of the Hindu world, all beings are obliged to experience each and every consequence of their actions. Those who don't experience these consequences in the same life have to experience them in the next. If the causal body is enlightened there are no consequences to experience; the body is liberated. In the absence of knowledge of the true self the causal body remains nothing but a bundle of ignorance. Such a causal body is reborn, pinning down the soul with it. Until it is time to reemerge in the land of the living, it waits in the land of the dead.

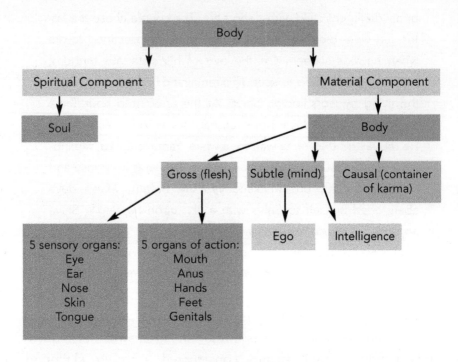

Structure of the Body

The land of the dead, known as Pitr-loka, is located across the fiery river Vaitarini that blocks the entry of gross and subtle bodies. Across the way the ancestors live under the watchful eye of Yama, a rather fierce and ruthless god. He is described as a dark being who rides a wild buffalo and holds a noose that separates the living causal body from the gross and subtle bodies.

⮂ The Death of Yama ⮀
(Rig Veda)

Yama was the son of the sun god Surya and was the first man. His sister Yami approached him and said they must lay together and produce children. Yama refused because they were siblings. As a result he died childless, and his sister mourned for him.

Yama has no hope of being reborn, for in the Hindu scheme

rebirth occurs when the children we leave behind in the land of the living have sex and reproduce. Yama, the first to enter the land of the dead, became the oldest forefather, and hence king of the ancestors. Yama is often addressed as Dharma, the keeper of order, for he selflessly and impersonally determines the circumstances governing our rebirth based on merits and demerits earned in our previous lives. He determines the gender and health of the new body as well as the nature of the family in which the rebirth will take place. His accountant, Chitragupta, maintains a strict account of all our deeds and misdeeds. Chitragupta is so strict that he is revered as the lord of accountants.

ᘓ Vishnu Cursed ᘒ
(Padma Purana)

Once Shukra, the guru of the demons, went on a pilgrimage. In taking advantage of his absence the gods attacked the demons, determined to vanquish them once and for all. The demons took refuge behind Shukra's mother, Kavyamata, who decided to chant a magic formula that would put all the gods to sleep until Shukra returned. Vishnu silenced her by slitting her throat with his discus. This ensured victory for the gods but earned Shukra's ire. Vishnu had committed the sin of killing a woman, the channel of rebirth. Shukra therefore cursed Vishnu with the experience of mortality. Thus a misdeed and the resulting demerit—regardless of his divine role in sustaining order on earth—forces Vishnu to incarnate on earth as Rama and Krishna and face death. No one can get past Yama's decree.

Hindu funerary rituals involve both fire and water. The dead body is cremated and the ashes cast in a river. The ritual has its foundation in the belief that there are two possible destinations after death: Yama-loka or Swarga-loka. Fire liberates the causal body; water binds it. Depending on the memories of past deeds, the jiva can either remain in samsara, oscillating between the land of the living and the land of the dead, or he or she can break free and end up in one of the many heavens of the Hindu mythosphere.

Hell, known as Naraka, did not originally exist in the Hindu mythosphere; the concept of hell is believed to have entered the mythosphere following contact with Persians, Muslims, and Christians. Like the biblical hell it is located underground, but must be distinguished from Patala, the abode of asuras and nagas. In Naraka, Yama punishes those who have not followed dharma.

In the Christian mythosphere souls wait in purgatory after death. On the day of judgment after Armageddon, when the forces of Satan have been vanquished, those who were true to God rise to heaven and the rest are damned for eternity in hell. Residence in Naraka is, however, not permanent. Like one's stay in Indra's paradise, a visit to Naraka is impermanent, ending when one has reaped the result of his karma.

Often tales from different mythospheres seem uncannily similar. Consider the following story, for example.

ᐁ Fish to the Rescue ᐃ
(Matsya Purana)

As the wheel of life moved into the Kali Yuga, the fourth and final quarter of existence, a very tired Brahma yawned. The Veda slipped out of his mouth and was stolen by the horse-headed asura Hayagriva. As a result the law of the jungle overtook the land. Righteous conduct was totally abandoned. Disorder was everywhere.

Amid the anarchy a compassionate ascetic called Manu, who had once been a king, rescued a small fish from a river and placed it in a pot. As the days passed, the fish kept growing, becoming too big to fit into a pot, a pond, a lake, or a river. Finally Manu released it into the sea. Not long after the oceans began to rise and submerge the earth. It was pralaya, the time when the aging world dies to make way for a new one.

The fish reappeared before Manu. It had grown so big that it covered the horizon. It had also sprouted a horn. The fish instructed Manu to place himself and the seven primal rishis, the seed of all animals and plants, on a boat. "Tie the boat to my horn and I will tow you to safety as the oceans wash away all that exists." While Manu organized the boat the fish found Hayagriva hiding in a shell under the sea. It killed the asura, reclaimed the Veda, and finally steered Manu and his boat through the terrifying tempest and into the eye of the storm at Mount Meru. There the Veda, the seed of human, plant, and animal, survived until the floodwaters receded.

CONCLUSION

The preceding story is a flood myth, just like the biblical story of Noah and the Mesopotamian myth of Ut-Napishtim. In all these stories the flood is the result of unrighteous behavior on earth. Only one good man survives the cataclysm to father the next, more righteous generation of humans. The common theme can be explained in two ways:

- The stories were either transmitted from one culture to another or they belong to a common past.
- The different cultures shared imagery from the common human unconscious where symbols emerge as a reaction to basic human experiences such as birth, death, fear, and insecurity.

The similarities, however, tend to overshadow the differences. The Mesopotamian and biblical floods are manifestations of divine rage, the decision of a council of gods known as Annunaki in one and the decision of God in another. But the Hindu flood is a predetermined event, like death. Divine will has very little to do with it. The Hindu flood myth recounts a recurring event, a function of time, an event that is bound to happen as the world goes through cycles of death and rebirth, just like every living creature. With every pralaya there is a fish to rescue and a Manu to rescue it. Thus the flood myth in Hindu narratives establishes a paradigm quite different from those of the Bible and Mesopotamian stories.

In the unique worldviews of all three stories water is associated with destruction while a mountain serves as a refuge. Water represents fluidity and flux. The mountain represents solidity, stability, and permanence. The people who revered these narratives shared the very human fear of change and sought deliverance from traumatic transitions. All sought a raft—the ark—to survive catastrophe. All hoped to find refuge in a palace that offered security.

Dissimilarities bring out the cultural understanding of a people. Similarities indicate their humanity.

❧ 3 ❧
Mythopoesis:
Transforming Myth

arratives, symbols, and rituals may appear to be communications of timeless truths, but they remain products of history, transforming—in form or in interpretation—with social, political, and cultural changes. If myth does not respond to reality it will stifle growth and immobilize culture, forcing its rejection by a community determined to move on.

Take, for example, the Hindu ritual of breaking coconuts or smashing pumpkins in ceremonies aimed at drawing benevolent forces into the household. This is a transactional ritual based on the law of karma: You give something to the cosmos to get something in return. At one time this ritual involved the sacrifice of animals, and probably even humans. The sacrificial victim was smeared with vermilion powder and turmeric paste, adorned with flowers and leaves, thanked by all the beneficiaries, and then beheaded with a single stroke of the hatchet so that death was instant and not painful (a suffering beast would curse the beneficiaries, thwarting the purpose of the ritual).

Following the rise of Buddhism and Jainism in the fifth century B.C.E., Indian society moved away from blood sacrifices and toward vegetarianism. The ritual had to change if it wanted to survive. The sacrifice became symbolic, with a coconut or a pumpkin substituting for an animal. The vermilion powder and turmeric paste remained, as did the injunction that the sacrifice be completed in one stroke. With time memory of the ritual's roots in blood sacrifice waned. A new reason was needed to continue the tradition. Mystical philosophies and doctrines of devotion came to the rescue. The act was seen as a symbolic breaking of the ego so that the individual can realize the divine. Thus as the community moved toward mystical ideals, vegetarianism, and the denial of material aspirations, the ritual was transformed both in form and meaning, all the while retaining its timeless quality.

In this chapter we shall see how Hindu narratives emerged, ideas evolved, and worldviews changed with history.

MARCH OF THE VEDIC HYMNS

All Hindus accept the Veda as the foundation of Hinduism. The Veda is made up of four collections of chants known as *mantras*. These chants are said to be authorless, eternal, timeless, and older and greater than the gods themselves. The mantras revealed themselves to seers known as rishis. When applied to a ritual known as yagna, mantra could manipulate the very functioning of the cosmos—ensure victory in battle, transform weapons into lethal missiles, make men virile and the land fertile.

In Vedic times, kings invited rishis to perform yagnas to solve temporal problems (see Fig. 2.1). The epic Ramayana informs us that Dasharatha, king of Ayodhya, had three wives but no sons. So he invited the sage Rishyashringa to perform a yagna. At the

end of the grand ritual, a being emerged from the fire altar holding a pot filled with a magic potion. "Whoever drinks from this
bowl will bear you a son," the being told Dasharatha. The king
divided the potion equally between Kaushalya, his senior queen,
and Kaikeyi, his favorite queen. The queens gave half their share
to Sumitra, the junior queen. Consequently, the three queens
gave birth to four sons. Kaushalya gave birth to Rama, Kaikeyi to
Bharata. Sumitra bore Lakshmana and Shatrughna. Lakshmana
was devoted to Rama, Shatrughna to Bharata.

The Vedic times were the ritualistic phase of Hinduism, the
Karma Kanda, when the concept of divinity rested not in the idea
of god but in the performance of ritual. The yagna was not merely
the means to appease divine beings and win their favor; it was an
end in itself that bestowed power even to the gods. Hence there
are narratives in which even gods needed rishis to perform the
yagna so that they could defeat their archenemies, the demons.

ᘉ The Beheading of Vishwarupa ᘉ (Mahabharata)

Indra, king of the gods, once annoyed his preceptor, Brihaspati,
who refused to perform a yagna in his name. Deprived of the ritual's power, Indra faced defeat at the hands of the demons.
Desperate, Indra sought the help of rishi Vishwarupa.
Unfortunately, this sage had a demon mother. So during the sacrifice, Vishwarupa made offerings to empower both the gods
and the demons. When Indra discovered this he beheaded
Vishwarupa.

With the power of mantra the rishi could transform ordinary
weapons into lethal missiles, make barren women pregnant, com-
pel the gods to do his bidding, and wander between celestial,
earthly, and subterranean realms, sometimes supporting and

sometimes opposing gods, humans, and demons. Rishis were therefore greatly revered.

⌘ Durvasa's Curse ⌘
(Padma Purana)

Rishi Durvasa gifted Indra with a celestial garland that the latter threw to the ground. Slighted, Durvasa cursed Indra that he would lose the grace of Shri, goddess of fortune. Instantly a pall of gloom descended on his kingdom. Trees bore neither flower nor fruit. Cows did not give milk. Indra's army was defeated in every battle.

Some rishis were addressed as *Prajapati,* which means "father of the people." But it has been suggested that the rishi did not really father races; he merely civilized them by bringing them into the Vedic fold.

That the yagna did not need a permanent structure for its performance suggests that the followers of the Vedic tradition were nomads or wanderers for many centuries before they settled down. There is much sociological and literary evidence to suggest that Vedic culture flourished around 1500 B.C.E. on the banks of a river called Saraswati that probably flowed west between the Indus and the Ganges. Then, scholars speculate, following climatic changes, a severe drought, or political upheaval, there was a migration of the Vedic tradition from northwest India (modern Pakistan) to the east (modern Bihar and Bengal) through the fertile Gangetic plains, and finally to the south of the Vindhya Mountains to the Tamil lands.

With this migration came stories of rishis traversing forests and hills. One sage who stands out is Agastya, who is accepted as the fountainhead of the southern Tamil tradition.

ᏨᏍ Mount Vindhya Bows ᏨᏍ
(Uttara Ramayana)

Once Shiva decided to give a discourse on the mysteries of the Vedas. Immediately all the rishis rushed to Shiva's abode in the Himalayas. This northward rush caused the earth to tilt. To restore the balance Shiva asked rishi Agastya to move south. When the sun god Surya saw Agastya moving south, he requested that the sage help him. "Mount Vindhya is trying to prove his superiority by growing taller each day," said Surya. "Now he has grown so tall that he almost blocks my path across the sky. Help me so that he grows no more." Agastya promised to help. As he approached the mountain, Vindhya bent down to salute him. "Maintain this posture," said Agastya. "I will be able to cross you with ease. And remain this way until I return so that I will have no trouble on my journey back." Agastya never returned north and Vindhya remained bent, enabling the sun to move with ease across the sky.

The Vindhya range divides the Indian subcontinent into northern and southern halves. Rishis who moved south associated the hills and rivers they came upon there with hills and rivers in the north through stories such as the following.

ᏨᏍ The Birth of River Kaveri ᏨᏍ
(Kaveri Mahatmya)

Agastya carried in a pot the waters of the river Ganges. This was a magical pot given by Shiva that was always full of the sacred water. There was a great drought in the south. To help his devotees the god Vinayaka took the form of a crow and tipped Agastya's water pot when he was not paying attention. From it gushed out the mighty Kaveri that irrigated the Tamil lands and brought prosperity wherever it went.

The migration of the guardians of Vedic culture to the south brought them in contact with many non-Vedic cultures, some of whom opposed them violently. Not surprisingly, in Vedic narratives, they have been identified as demons, though the word *barbarian* would be more appropriate.

⤙ Repelling Taraka ⤚
(Ramayana)

Rishi Vishwamitra, who was conducting a yagna in the forest, was being harassed by rakshasas who threw blood and bones to contaminate the fire altar and disrupt the proceedings. Exasperated, Vishwamitra approached Dasharatha, king of Ayodhya, who deputed his son Rama to rid the forest of these vile barbarians. Rama was a skillful archer. His arrows kept the rakshasas at bay while Vishwamitra completed the sacrifice. Pleased, the sage gave Rama mantras that could transform his arrows into deadly missiles.

The epic Ramayana is sometimes viewed as a documentation of the confrontation between Vedic and non-Vedic ways of life as the Vedic culture moved south. In it monkeys and vultures help the hero Rama (see Fig. 2.2).

⤙ Rama Befriends the Monkeys ⤚
(Ramayana)

Ravana, king of the rakshasas, abducted Rama's wife, Sita, while he was away on a hunt. A vulture called Jatayu who had witnessed the abduction tried in vain to stop Ravana, who chopped off his wings. As he breathed his last breath, Jatayu informed Rama that Ravana had taken Sita southward. As Rama wandered south in search of Sita, he came upon a band of monkeys led by Sugriva. They had been driven out of the monkey kingdom Kishkinda by the monkey king Vali following a misunderstanding.

Fig 2.1. Rishis performing yagnas to appease celestial beings and influence temporal events (North Indian miniature, eighteenth century). More on page 116.

Fig 2.2. Rama, upholder of Vedic ways, befriending the monkeys as he journeyed south in search of his wife, who had been abducted by the king of barbarians (Andhra painting, nineteenth century). More on page 120.

Fig 2.3. Shiva, though the ascetic form of God, is depicted wearing the sacred thread to associate him with the socially dominant caste of brahmanas (calendar art, twentieth century). More on page 127.

Fig 2.4. *Parashurama of the priest caste dismembering Kartaviryarjuna of the warrior caste for stealing his cow (Mysore painting, twentieth century). More on page 127.*

Fig 2.5. Shiva giving his discourse to sages, thereby becoming Adi-nath, the primal guru (South Indian temple wall carving, twentieth century). More on page 131.

Fig 2.6. The apsara was the water nymph who facilitated fertility and opposed asceticism (Orissan temple carving, twelfth century). More on page 136.

Fig 2.7. Skanda or Kartikeya, the hypermasculine boy-god, who was born after Shiva's seed was incubated in several wombs (calendar art, twentieth century. More on page 137.

Fig 2.8. *Krishna, who is God, raises Mount Govardhana to serve as a parasol and humble Indra, the Vedic rain god (North Indian miniature, nineteenth century). More on page 141.*

Fig 2.9. Shiva who uses dance as a medium of enlightenment (Chola bronze from Tamil Nadu, twentieth century). More on page 145.

Fig 2.10. Mallikarjuna, a parochial manifestation of the cosmic Shiva worshippe in parts of South India (calendar art, twentieth century). More on page 147.

Fig 2.11. Vishnu as the wily teacher who deluded demons into giving up the Vedas (Mysore painting, twentieth century). More on page 150.

Fig 2.12. Ayyappa, a tribal god who was absorbed into mainstream Hinduism where he became known as the son of Shiva and Vishnu (calendar art, twentieth century). More on page 151.

Fig 2.13. Kalki, the Hindu messiah who will destroy wrongdoers and restore order (Mysore painting, twentieth century). More on page 155.

Fig 2.14. Krishna, the god of herdsmen, dancing on the hood of Kaliya, a serpent, who was probably a god of farmers (Chola bronze from Tamil Nadu, twentieth century). More on page 164.

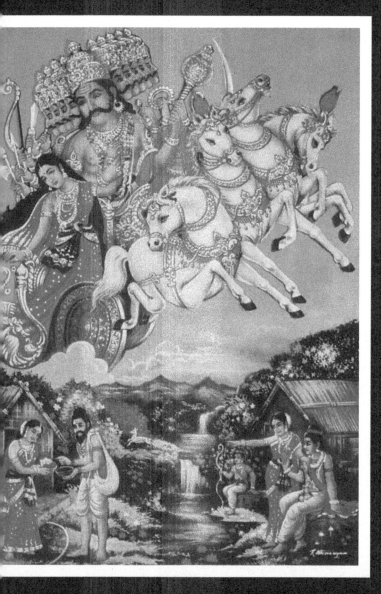

Fig 2.15. Shiva shooting a missile to bring down the three flying saucers, which were cities that were inhabited by demons (Mysore painting, twentieth century). More on page 173.

Fig 2.16. The abduction of Sita by Ravana who rode a flying chariot (calendar art, twentieth century). More on page 174.

Fig 2.17. *The restless Lakshmi sits domesticated at Vishnu's feet (Ganjifa painting, eighteenth century). More on page 177.*

Fig 2.18. Sati, the chaste widow who burns herself on her husband's funeral pyre, is revered by traditionalists but challenged by modern reformers (calendar art, twentieth century). More on page 178.

Fig 2.19. Temple images of Krishna (right) with his brother (left) and sister (center) at Puri, Orissa, look malformed and probably have tribal totemic origins according to anthropologists (calendar art, twentieth century). More on page 182.

Fig 2.20. Lakshmi, the goddess of fortune, is worshipped in virtually every
Hindu household and business establishment (palm-leaf painting from
Orissa, twentieth century). More on page 186.

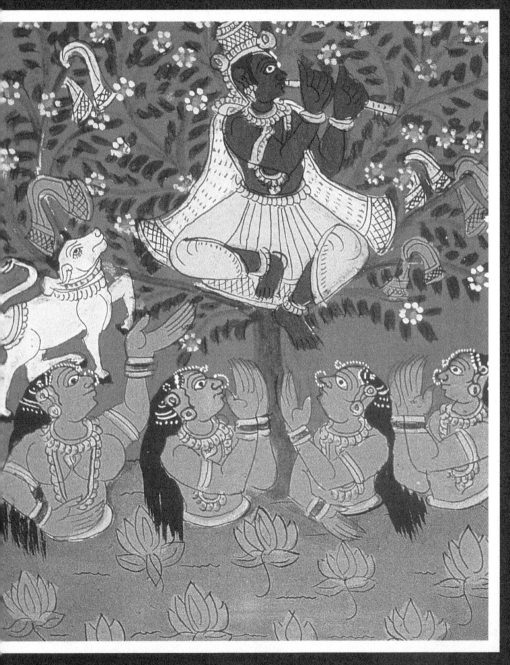

Fig 2.21. *Krishna stealing clothes of milkmaids bathing in a river, a prank that devotees prefer to interpret allegorically (Andhra painting, twentieth century). More on page 188.*

Fig 2.22. The Shri-chakra a potent fertility symbol that geometrically conveys Hindu metaphysical ideas (Harish Johari, from Tools for Tantra, *published 1986 by Destiny Books, Rochester, Vermont). More on page 194.*

Rama helped Sugriva kill Vali and become king of the monkeys. Sugriva in turn ordered his subjects to help Rama. They located Sita to the island of Lanka, built a bridge across the sea, launched an attack on the rakshasa kingdom, overthrew Ravana, and rescued Sita.

The word used for monkey in the epic is *vanara*. The word has been traced to the words *vana*, meaning "forest," and *nara*, meaning "man," thus suggesting that the vanaras were not monkeys but rather tribes whose totem was a monkey. Likewise, Jatayu was probably not a vulture but a tribe whose totem was a bird. The author of the epic probably identified non-Vedic tribes rather contemptuously as being animals since they seemed to follow the law of the jungle (might is right), unlike the protagonist Rama who followed the Vedic code of duty before happiness.

The followers of the Vedic tradition were identified as manavas, descendents of Manu, who was the first man and the first Vedic king. *Manava* also means "human," suggesting that in the Vedic tradition one was believed to be less than human, and hence animal or demon, if one did not follow Manu's Vedic way. Another word used for followers of the Vedic way was *arya*, the "noble one." In recent times, the word *arya* has been influenced by the Nazi discourse and has unfortunately become a racial term.

As more lands came under the Vedic fold, forests were cleared to make way for cities. The epic Mahabharata justifies this encroachment by calling it an offering to the fire god.

ᨆ The Burning of Khandavaprastha ᨆ (Mahabharata)

The Pandavas had inherited the wilderness of Khandavaprastha, where they planned to build a city. The fire god Agni promised to help them if they allowed him to feed on the flora and fauna of the forest. The Pandavas agreed, and Agni's flames soon engulfed the forest. All the residents—birds, beasts, demons, and serpents—were burned in the conflagration. The Pandavas shot all those who tried to escape. They even created a canopy of arrows over the forest so that the rain god Indra, who had been summoned by the beasts, could not put out Agni's flames. The asura Mara begged the Pandavas to spare him and his family; in return he promised to build them a fabulous city.

The burning of the forest to build a settlement was a common practice in Vedic times, one that resulted in conflict with forest dwellers. Sometimes a compromise was reached, as the following story of the Prachetasa brothers relates. In the story the underwater sojourn probably refers to an expedition of manavas on the sea during which the forest dwellers killed those who had been left behind.

ೲ The Marriage of Marisha ೲ
(Bhagavata Purana)

The ten Prachetasa brothers spent years meditating under the sea. After gaining a vision of Vishnu they rose to find the earth covered with trees. They spat out fire to clear the overgrowth. The trees begged them to stop and gave them the hand of their foster daughter Marisha in marriage.

Based on the fragmentary evidence found in many narratives, some have suggested that during a great famine or flood, probably the one that caused the Vedic culture to move south, the Vedas were lost. Rishi Vyasa, whose name means the "compiler," restored it for the benefit of humanity. Manuals known as Brahmanas were put together to show how chants were to be applied to ritual. The human custodian of these manuals was known as the brahmana.

As keepers of Vedic lore, brahmanas became well versed in Vaastu, the science of space; Jyotisha, the science of time; Ayurveda, the science of healing; Vedangas, the science to interpret the Vedas; and Puranas, the chronicles of gods, kings, and sages. Brahmanas served as the link between the material and spiritual realms. They knew the secrets of the cosmos. Just as Brihaspati was the spiritual guide of the devas and Shukra the spiritual guide of the asuras, the brahmana established himself in the court of kings.

With the spread of Vedic culture as peoples, communities, and tribes mingled and merged, the Vedic brahmanas tried to retain their superior position and their spiritual purity by not sharing food or their daughters with nonbrahmanas. Their patrons, the ruling class, also adopted this practice. Eventually the priests consolidated a social organism that depended on four groups known as *varna* for its survival. This fourfold division of society was considered divinely ordained.

☙ The Body of Society ☙
(Rig Veda)

Purusha, the organism that is society, has for a head the brahmanas (priests and philosophers who are involved in religious activity), for hands the kshatriyas (kings, noblemen, and warriors who are involved in defense and administration), for the thighs and groin the vaishya (farmers, herdsmen, and traders who are involved in economic activity), and for feet the shudra (craftsmen and laborers who serve society).

Ideally, the varna system should have organized society, brought about division of labor, and prevented any one group from being overly exploited. In reality, however, the division created a hierarchy with the brahmana positioning himself above all. Society could live without arms, without thighs, and without feet, but not without its head.

Over time each varna divided and subdivided itself based on many factors, mainly occupation, ancestry, and geographical location. Each of these groups was known as a *jati,* or caste. Intermingling, especially intermarriage, between members of different jati was frowned upon. The balance of power between castes waxed and waned depending on economics and politics. At all times the priest remained atop the varna pyramid.

As custodians of ancient scriptures, brahmanas had the power to interpret narratives to their own advantage. They equated themselves with rishis even though one became rishi by effort and not by birth.

∾ Vishwamitra Becomes a Rishi ∾
(Bhagavata Purana)

King Kaushika tried to claim Vasistha's cow by force. But the rishi repelled his army with the power of mantra. Determined to defeat Vasistha, Kaushika decided to become a rishi himself. He abandoned his kingdom and his crown, went to the forest, and performed austerities, and after many years became a rishi well versed in the secrets of the Veda.

Since the caste system established the brahmanas' superiority in society, they endorsed the system enthusiastically. In the following story Drona belongs to the brahmana caste and earns his living by teaching the martial arts to the princes of the powerful Kuru clan. He safeguards the interests of his patrons and his caste ruthlessly.

∾ Ekalavya ∾
(Mahabharata)

Drona, the teacher of the Kuru princes, refused to teach archery to Ekalavya, as he was of tribal origin. Since he was determined to learn Ekalavya built an effigy of Drona and taught himself to wield the bow in its shadow. In time he became so adept at archery that he could shoot arrows into the mouth of a barking dog, silencing it without causing any injury. Ekalavya was clearly more skilled than the Kuru princes. In all humility, Ekalavya attributed his success to his belief that Drona was his guru. "If you think I am your guru then it is your duty to give me my fee. I charge you the thumb of the hand with which you hold your bow." Ekalavya was horrified with this demand, which would prevent him from holding the bow ever again, but he complied nevertheless.

When the Kuru princes asked their guru to explain his cruelty he said, "If everybody learns archery then tribals will replace kshatriyas and the entire varna edifice will collapse, leading to social anarchy. Besides, I had promised Arjuna that none of my students would be better than him at archery. By destroying Ekalavya I have kept that promise."

People feared the power the brahmana possessed because of his knowledge of the Veda. Everything was done to appease him. Cows and daughters were given to him as gifts. He was never taxed or punished, even when he committed a crime. In fact, killing brahmanas was deemed a crime against the cosmos because they were receptacles of the Veda.

⤳ Atoning for Killing Ravana ⤳
(Rishikesh Sthala Purana)

After Rama killed Ravana, the villain who had abducted his wife, he went on a pilgrimage to atone for the sin of killing a brahmana; for Ravana, king of rakshasas, was a brahmana. His father was the rishi Vaishrava, and Ravana was well versed in the Veda. Rama, the son of a king, thus stood lower than Ravana in the caste heirarchy.

Narratives arose showing how even divine beings preferred association with the upper castes.

∾ Ammaveru's Husband ∾
(South Indian folklore)

Ammaveru's father gave her in marriage to a man he thought was a brahmana. But one day Ammaveru saw the man eating beef with his mother. Upon realizing that a low-caste man had duped her, Ammaveru transformed into a fiery goddess and killed him.

Every effort was made to associate folk heroes with the upper castes.

∾ The Birth of Krishna ∾
(Harivamsa)

Everyone wondered why Krishna, the son of the cowherd chieftain Nanda and his wife Yashoda, was dark while his parents were fair. The truth was known only to a select few. Krishna was the eighth son of the Yadava nobleman Vasudeva and his wife, Devaki, who was destined to kill Kamsa, dictator of Mathura. Warned of this by oracles, Kamsa had killed every child that Devaki had given birth to.

To save this child the goddess Yogamaya cast the spell of sleep on the city of Mathura the night Krishna was born. On her advice, Vasudeva took the child across the river Yamuna and exchanged him with the daughter of Nanda. When Kamsa tried to kill this girl child she transformed into a goddess who declared that Kamsa's killer was safe and being reared far away from his murderous hands.

In images gods were depicted with a sacred thread worn over the left shoulder across the trunk—the distinguishing mark of a brahmana (see Fig. 2.3). Brahmanas were clearly using their pivotal roles to dominate society.

A child born into the caste of the brahmanas was given access to Vedic lore only after he had undergone the thread ceremony, during which he was born again through the womb of his teacher. Although God transcends caste, human manifestations of the divine are always visualized with the sacred thread of the brahmana hanging over the right shoulder.

THE ASCETIC IDEAL

Around 500 B.C.E. there was a growing restlessness against Vedic ritualism and Brahmanical domination. Kings, the erstwhile patrons of fire-churning priests, questioned the pivotal position of brahmanas in society. This led to conflict and often violent confrontation.

ᨳ Parashurama Destroys the Warrior Race ᨳ (Vishnu Purana)

The rishi Jamadagni had a cow that could fulfill every desire. She was given to him by the Haihaiyas as a fee for Jamadagni's services as a priest. Years later the king of the Haihaiyas, Kartaviryarjuna, reclaimed this miraculous cow and tried to take her away by force. Reclaiming alms was against the code of dharma. The rishi's protests fell on deaf years. Finally the rishi's youngest son, Parashurama, could take it no more. Abandoning the nonviolent ways of his family, he raised an axe, blocked the path of the king, challenged him to a fight, and in the duel that followed hacked him to death. Kartaviryarjuna's son reacted by raiding the hermitage a few days later and beheading Jamadagni. In a fury Parashurama swore to teach the caste of warriors the price of abandoning dharma in a language they understood. In the massacre that followed Parashurama killed five generations of warriors to fill five great lakes with their blood (see Fig. 2.4).

Brahmanical domination upset the balance of power not just with kings but also with the newly emerging class of traders, who felt that rituals were destroying valuable wealth without addressing the issues that affected the common person. Questions were raised through narratives on the value of ritual over reality.

༄ The Golden Mongoose ༄
(Mahabharata)

A poor man let his family starve to death so that a stranger who had sought his hospitality could eat. A mongoose slipped and fell in the serving bowl. The half of the animal that came in contact with the leftovers turned golden. Realizing that this was the power of sacrifice, the mongoose traveled around the world looking for another equally potent sacrifice so that the rest of his body could become golden. He heard of a grand yagna being conducted by Yudhishtira where thousands were being fed. At the end of the ceremony the half-golden mongoose entered the sacrificial precinct and rubbed its other half with ashes from the fire altar. Nothing happened. The mongoose concluded that the heartfelt sacrifice of a poor man had more power than grand ritualistic sacrifices of kings.

There were disagreements between brahmanas themselves on the truth of the Veda. Some, like Yagnavalkya, saw the mantras as spiritual rather than ritual tools. They shifted the focus from the world outside to the world within. Rather than using rituals to manipulate the world, they questioned humans' attitude to the world and the reasons for it.

ᥰᥱ Yagnavalkya Rebels ᥲᥰ
(Brahmanda Purana)

Rishi Vaisampayana had killed his nephew. He asked his students to perform a ritual to rid him of the demerits emerging from that act. Yagnavalkya refused, as he believed that atonement came from true remorse, not ritual action. Outraged, Vaisampayana demanded that Yagnavalkya return what was taught to him and leave the hermitage. Yagnavalkya did so, vomiting up the Yajur Veda he had learned from his master. The other students took the form of black birds and pecked at it. What they acquired thus came to be known as Black Yajur Veda, which is much cruder in form than the White Yajur Veda put together by Yagnavalkya after he learned the scriptures once again from the sun god himself.

Kings such as Janaka invited sages such as Yagnavalkya to debate the true reality of the cosmos. The debates and discussions inspired the Upanishads, a collection of commentaries that gave rise to a philosophy known as Vedanta, considered the acme of Vedic thought. In it the Hindu ideas of samsara, karma, dharma, and moksha were consolidated. A new age was emerging, one in which yoga, the control of mental processes, once viewed as esoteric and marginal, became part of the mainstream.

ᥰᥱ Nachiketa Questions Yama ᥲᥰ
(Katha Upanishad)

Nachiketa wanted to know if there was life after death, so he questioned Yama, the god of death. After much persuasion Yama said that even the gods do not know the answer, but he would try. He said that what dies is the body, not the soul, which is eternal. Being enchanted by the material world, or samsara, our minds believe that the ego, a transitory product of external impressions, is our true identity. This false identification makes us react to various sensory stimuli in a manner that pleases the ego. Because, by the cosmic law of karma, all creatures are obliged to experience the reactions of all their actions, either in this life or the next, the soul gets dragged through a series of lives, each time fettered within a body and in circumstances determined by past actions. Liberation, or moksha, stems from the realization that the soul is our true identity. Realization comes only when the mind is trained by yoga to transcend desire, follow the code of dharma, overpower the ego, and outgrow the seduction of material things that are ephemeral anyway.

Karma was used to explain the caste one was born into and the events that occurred in life. Stories emerged of how karma affected the gods themselves.

༄ Vidura's Past Life ༄
(Mahabharata)

While the sage Mandavya meditated, a thief entered his hermitage. When the king's soldiers caught the thief they concluded that the sage had given the thief shelter. For this crime Mandavya was tortured and impaled. A day later the sage's innocence was proven and he was let go. Mandavya went to Dharma, god of justice, to learn what had he done to suffer torture at the hands of the soldiers. Dharma said that this was the result of torturing bees as a child. Mandavya lost his temper, as he felt the innocent actions of a child do not merit such a harsh reaction. He cursed Dharma to be born as Vidura, the son of a slave, who though worthy of kingship would never wear the crown because of his inferior birth.

With the rise of ideas such as karma and moksha, society veered away from ritualism toward philosophy, asceticism, monasticism, and mysticism. Yagna was sidelined in favor of deliberation, renunciation, isolation, contemplation, meditation, and prayer. The nonritualists believed that the true power of Vedic hymns lay not in their application to yagna, but in their understanding. Thus the age of speculation, or Gyan Kanda, the intellectual phase of Hinduism, came into being, during which attitude and understanding mattered more than action.

With new ideas came new spiritual practices such as tapasya, a complex mixture of yoga, self-denial, self-introspection, meditation, and contemplation. Ascetic figures appeared in narratives who outshone yagna-performing priests. They were addressed variously as *muni* (he who contemplates silently) or *tapasvin* (he who performs tapasya). They rejected worldly life, isolated themselves in forests and caves, and subjected themselves to extreme austerity in the quest to understand the workings of the cosmos. Their path needed no patron, no priest, no altar, and no offering. It was a private and personal endeavor, not a public spectacle.

Fragmentary passage in the Veda suggests that asceticism was not merely the consequence of restlessness with ritualism, but, in fact, a parallel movement. While the priests and their royal patrons performed yagna, the vaishya and the sudra were ignored. For their spiritual needs the lay people worshipped the spirits of the animal, plant, and mineral worlds. They also took guidance from wandering hermits and mysterious holy men who lived in caves and forests and possessed magical powers. They were the *natha,* or masters of magic, sorcery, and alchemy. They provided the farmer, the herdsman, and the rest of the laity with charms and talismans and hymns to harness benevolent natural forces and ward off malevolent ones. Their wisdom was attributed to Shiva, who was the primal guru Adi-nath (see Fig. 2.5). In later Hinduism Shiva was worshipped as Mahadeva, God who is greater than the Vedic gods.

ᏚᏍ Shiva Enlightens Matsyendra-nath ᏚᏍ
(Nav-Nath-Charitra)

Shiva once shared his wisdom with his consort Parvati in secret on the banks of a river far away from all human settlements. A fish in the river overheard the conversation and was enlightened. The wisdom transformed the fish into a human being and a sage called Matsyendra-nath or the "fish-master." He went about finding nine disciples, who collectively came to be known as *nav-nath* or the nine masters. They passed Shiva's wisdom on to the rest of humanity.

In hindsight the teachings of the Nath tradition were described as Tantra, and by most followers of the tantric tradition, Shiva was considered to be the primal teacher. The power tantric knowledge bestowed was known as *siddhi,* but to possess it the aspirant had to submit himself to numerous psycho-physical practices known as yoga. These involved challenging social norms and cultural taboos and could not be practiced by householders. Masters accepted as students men (and occasionally women) who were willing to renounce mainstream society. Tantra and yoga formed the foundation of many folk fertility rituals but eventually were absorbed into mainstream monastic orders. The following narrative captures the tensions between the exoteric Vedic rituals and the esoteric tantric practices.

ᏚᏍ The Destruction of Daksha's Yagna ᏚᏍ
(Skanda Purana)

Prajapati Daksha's daughter had married the devas. But the youngest daughter, Sati, had chosen to marry the mendicant Shiva against her father's wishes. Daksha did not like Shiva, as the mendicant did not respect the code of civilization and the hierarchies of society. To teach his son-in-law a lesson, Daksha conducted a yagna and invited everyone but Shiva. When Sati learned of her father's intention she strode into the sacrificial precinct and leaped into the fire pit, killing herself and contaminating the altar so that the ritual ground to a halt.

When Shiva learned of Sati's death he was so angry that he commanded all his followers to attack and destroy Daksha's yagna. Shiva's hordes destroyed everything in sight and drove out the assembled guests. In the midst of the pandemonium Virabhadra beheaded Daksha while Kali cackled in glee. The gods begged Shiva to forgive them. Finally, after much appeasement, Shiva gave in. He restored Daksha to life and the yagna commenced. This time an offering was made to Shiva, who continued to wander outside the perimeter of culture.

For the common man asceticism was less about understanding the universe and more about controlling it. Even Vedic tapasvins were viewed not merely as mystics or sages but also as magicians and sorcerers who could harm or heal with a touch or a glance.

ᑫᔆ Kapila's Fiery Glance ᑫᔆ
(Ramayana)

King Sagara had performed 999 horse sacrifices. If he succeeded in performing the thousandth sacrifice he would become more powerful than the gods. To prevent this the gods stole the sacrificial horse and hid it in the cave where Kapila was performing tapasya. When Sagara's sons found the horse, they accused Kapila of theft. Kapila was so furious that he abandoned his tapas and opened his eyes. His glance incinerated Sagara's sons, who were reduced to ashes.

Often the ascetic was addressed as a rishi, for tapasya was believed to be yagna internalized. Rishis like Agastya, Brishpaspati, and Shukra performed yagna and practiced tapasya. Like the ritual, this ascetic practice could make a man as powerful as a god.

ᘓᔢ Trishanku ᔢᘓ
(Vishnu Purana)

While Vishwamitra was away performing tapasya, a great drought swept the land. An outcast called Trishanku saved Vishwamitra's family from starvation by feeding them beef. In gratitude Vishwamitra agreed to fulfill Trishanku's deepest desire: to enter heaven with his mortal body. With the power of tapasya, he made Trishanku rise heavenward. The gods, however, prevented Trishanku's entry into paradise on the grounds that he was too polluted by being an outcast and because he killed and ate cows.

As he was determined to have his way Vishwamitra prevented Trishanku from returning to earth. Since his powers matched Indra's, Trishanku remained suspended in midair. Enraged, Vishwamitra declared his intention to redesign the cosmos and create a heaven only for Trishanku. Peace was restored and a compromise reached when the gods agreed to let Trishanku hang his head downward as a constellation in the starry sky.

While only a member of the brahmana caste was qualified by birth to perform yagna, tapasya was open to all. Narratives emerged describing the tapasya of various beings, including gods, humans, animals, demons, and barbarians.

ᘓᔢ Kumbhakarna's Asceticism ᔢᘓ
(Ramayana)

Kumbhakarna the rakshasa performed severe austerities to obtain from Brahma, father of all beings, a boon. Since Kumbhakarna was already strong enough to defeat celestial beings, the devas were terrified of what he might ask. So they requested that Saraswati, the goddess of speech, twist Kumbhakarna's tongue. As a result, instead of asking for more strength Kumbhakarna asked for more sleep. Brahma decreed, "You will sleep all the time." When Kumbhakarna realized his mistake he requested that Brahma undo the damage. Since boons cannot be taken back, only modified, Brahma said, "You will wake up once a year, and on that day you will be invincible. But should you be awakened on any other day, you will die."

Ascetics did not care for social divisions and hierarchy. Those who did not get access to Vedic secrets through yagna-performing priests often sought the help of hermits.

ᐁ Dadhichi's Head ᐅ
(Jaiminya Brahmana)

The gods refused to share the secret of the Veda with the Ashwini twins. They declared that the head of anyone who revealed the secret would burst into a thousand pieces. The Ashwini twins went to the ascetic Dadhichi, who was willing to share the secret with them. He told the twins to replace his head with that of a horse. After he had revealed all, as per divine decree, the equine head burst and the twins replaced his human head. Thus the Ashwini twins learned the secret of the Veda without killing Dadhichi.

With the passage of time people increasingly believed that the power obtained through tapasya was greater than power obtained through yagna.

ᐁ Dadhichi's Bones ᐅ
(Mahabharata)

Indra once killed a rishi called Vishwarupa. News of this murder reached Vishwarupa's father, Tvastha, who performed a yagna, invoked an asura called Vritra, and ordered him to annihilate Indra's armies. The only weapon with which Vritra could be killed was one made of the bones of Dadhichi, a hermit whose bones had been energized by tapasya. On Indra's request the sage Dadhichi abandoned his body and let the devas fashion a weapon with his bones with which Indra killed Vritra.

The rise of ascetic traditions marked the waning of the great Vedic ritual the yagna and the rise of the monastic ideal. Tapasya and yoga were grounded in the newly evolving metaphysics. This new theory held that energy that enlivens the body dissipates when humans succumb to desire; if retained through asceticism it can transform into fiery spiritual energy with which humans can control the cosmos. Carnal temptation was the greatest threat to the acquisition of this power. This idea was reflected in the many stories involving ascetics and nymphs.

Apsaras were water nymphs who entertained the gods and represented the sensual delights of life (see Fig. 2.6). The gods, suspicious of ascetic power, often used the apsaras to distract hermits and destroy their tapasya. The most famous confrontation of all occurred between Vishwamitra and Menaka.

☙ Vishwamitra and Menaka ❧
(Bhagavata Purana)

Vishwamitra was determined to gain spiritual power, so he retired to the forest where he meditated, sitting motionless like a rock until termites built a hill around him. Fearing the power Vishwamitra might acquire, Indra sent the divine damsel Menaka to seduce the ascetic. She succeeded. But failure did not stop Vishwamitra from trying again. This time the arrival of nymphs did not distract the king. He acquired the spiritual powers and became as renowned a rishi as Vasistha.

The association of woman with temptation and all things material sparked monastic thoughts in Hindu society. The Vedic rishi was very much a married man. Brihaspati, Shukra, Kasyapa, and Agastya all had wives and children. Unmarried people could not perform the yagna. Tapasya and yoga, on the other hand, demanded suppression of carnal thoughts and veered away from conjugal relationships. The tapasvin was not a family man; he was a renouncer. Narratives emerged expressing the tension between the householder's life and that of the renouncer, between the joy found with women and the power acquired without them.

ᴄᴧ The Seduction of Rishyashringa ᴄᴧᴐ
(Mahabharata)

Rishyashringa's father never allowed him to see a woman. This enforced chastity made Rishyashringa so powerful that one day when a downpour drenched him, he cursed the skies and prevented rain from falling on the ground. The only way to break the curse was to make him lose his chastity and hence his powers. So King Lomaharsha sent his daughter Shanta to seduce the innocent sage. Rishyashringa succumbed in no time. With his power gone, it began to rain once again.

The idea that association with women weakens the body led to the rise of hypermasculine heroes who were *ayonija*—not born of a womb—and who distanced themselves from women.

One of those heroes, Skanda, commander of the celestial armies, god of war, and lord of the planet Mars, is associated with symbols of heightened masculinity: He bears a lance, rides a peacock that pins down a serpent (feminine symbol), and holds a banner with the emblem of a rooster (see Fig. 2.7).

ᴄᴧ The Birth of Skanda ᴄᴧᴐ
(Skanda Purana)

Skanda was born of Shiva's semen, which had remained unshed for eons. As incubation in a womb would have made Skanda mortal, the gods ensured that Shiva shed his seed outside his consort's body. So fiery was the seed that even the fire god could not hold it. Neither Vayu, the wind god, nor Ganga, the river nymph, could cool it. Finally the seed set a marsh on fire. Within the embers the seed transformed into a six-headed child that was nursed by six forest nymphs called Krittikas. When he was barely six days old the hypermasculine child was strong and virile enough to kill the demon Taraka.

The age of speculation saw the subservience of woman to man. She was deified if she submitted totally to the will of her husband. To be chaste and faithful was the only dharma of woman.

∽ Shilavati's Chastity ∽
(Brahmanda Purana)

Shilavati's husband was a leper. Still she looked at no other man. One day her husband expressed his desire to visit a courtesan. Since he could not walk Shilavati carried him to the brothel on her shoulders. A sage who saw this was so disgusted that he uttered a curse: Shilavati's husband would die before sunset. When Shilavati heard this she was so distressed that she used the power of her chastity and prevented the sun from setting. With great difficulty was Shilavati persuaded to release the sun. When she finally let the sun rise, her husband died.

Several monastic orders emerged in India in the period following the disillusionment with Vedic ritualism. They could be classified into two groups: those who relied on the Veda in their quest for the truth and those who did not. The latter path was known as the path of the *shramana* or "strivers," to distinguish them from the brahmana, who clung to the Veda. The shramana gave empirical observation and meditation more importance than thoughts expressed in Vedic chants. Unlike earlier monks, the shramana did not retreat into forests. He shared his ideas with the laity, addressing issues that mattered to the masses, communicating with them in colloquial tongues. The common man—the farmer, herdsman, artisan, and trader—tired of being sidelined in the Vedic scheme of things, found great comfort in the words of the shramana.

Two monastic orders emerged out of the shramana revolution: the Buddhists and the Jains. Buddhists prescribed meditation and contemplation to cope with the problems of life. Jains suggested austerity and nonviolence. Both threatened the very existence of Vedic culture in India, forcing it to redefine itself.

THE BIRTH OF GOD

Vedic brahmanas deemed the Buddhists and Jains *nastika,* or non-believers, because they did not accept the Veda as the repository of cosmic truths. Eventually the word *nastika* came to mean "atheist." To believe in the Veda was to believe in God—so said the brahmana. This move from ritualism and speculation to theism was a deliberate one. It transformed Vedism into Hinduism and ensured that the latter became the dominant religion of the land.

Buddhism and Jainism were fundamentally monastic orders; their ultimate aim was liberation from the conundrums of material existence. Though appealing in principle, they made too many intellectual and disciplinary demands on the laity, most of whom were inclined toward but not fixated on mystical goals. Common people were unwilling to forsake their material aspirations. It was easier to adore spiritual masters than to follow their monastic teachings. So the monk was revered, even worshipped, but not emulated. Even the monks developed a condescending attitude toward the laity, considering them as nothing more than almsgivers who supported their spiritual growth. An unspoken chasm opened between the monastery and the mainstream.

The laity returned to the spiritual practice it had always been comfortable with: invocation, adoration, appeasement, and worship of spirits who animated the plant, animal, and mineral worlds. This quasi-animistic tradition is called the folk, or *desi,* tradition to distinguish it from the classical *margi* Vedic-Brahmanical traditions (see Table 25).

TABLE 25. COMPARISON OF THE CLASSICAL AND FOLK TRADITIONS OF HINDUISM

	Classical Tradition	Folk Tradition
AIM OF RITUALS	Propitiate divine beings, maintain order, and attain liberation	Harness the bounty of nature and draw its favorable energies into the household
APPROACH	Cosmic	Parochial
MOVEMENT OF IDEOLOGY	From the upper to the lower strata of society	From the lower to the upper strata of society
PHILOSOPHY	Vedic (Nigama)	Tantric (Agama)
TILT	Monastic orders (philosophy and mysticism)	Fertility rites (occult and magic)
ULTIMATE AIM	Order in society, liberation from worldly problems	Pleasure, prosperity, and power
VISION	Heavenward	Earthbound
WORLDVIEW	All reality is a divine delusion (maya)	All reality is divine power (shakti)

Since they were kept away from Vedic rituals and overlooked in margi or classical speculation, common people had always found refuge in earthbound gods, in narratives of heroes and ancestors who protected the boundaries of settlements, in household rituals rousing the fertility of the village goddess, and in the charms and chants of the esoteric and occult visions of wandering mystics, sorcerers, and alchemists (such as yogis, tantrikas, nathas, and siddhas). The folk deities—ammas, matas, matrikas, mahavidyas, yoginis, rakshasas, yakshas, nagas, vanaras, ganas, apsaras, gandharvas, bhutas, pretas, and pisachas—existed on the tongues of bards, in the shrines of the common man, in forests, in fields, on thresholds, on riverbanks, atop mountains, inside caves, beside lakes, and within homes. Some were revered, some adored, some appeased, and some supplicated. Through gifts and sacrifices their intervention was sought and their interference evaded.

Scriptures from the age of rituals referred to the earth- and water-bound divinities of the masses occasionally and often disdainfully, as they did not appeal to the celestial visions of the priests and their patrons. But they made their power felt in the age of speculation, when the brahmana priest and the shramana monk realized that for all their intellectual speculation, it was this mythology that kept the common person in thrall. Only a discourse that successfully accommodated this mythology would win the hearts of all. The age of speculation saw the rise of popular narratives, the Hindu Puranas, and the Buddhist Jatakas; hence it is also called the age of epics. In these stories popular folk heroes such as Krishna overpowered Vedic gods such as Indra (see Fig. 2.8).

৩ Krishna Humbles Indra ৩
(Bhagavata Purana)

Krishna told the cowherds to worship Mount Govardhana instead of Indra, god of rain, because this hill prevented rain-bearing clouds from going elsewhere and its slopes served as pastures for their cows. The cowherds did as they were told, annoying Indra, who sent down torrential rains to flood the village of cowherds and drown their cows. To save his people and their cattle, Krishna lifted Mount Govardhana and held it up like a parasol with his little finger. Realizing he was no match for Krishna, Indra apologized for his audacity and stopped the rain.

It was to the spirits and deities who controlled the plant, animal, and mineral worlds that the common people returned after their tryst with the monastic ideal. This was a return informed by mystical possibilities. Life was not just about righteous conduct (dharma), materialistic pursuits (artha), and sensuous activities (kama); it was also about breaking free from the fetters of earthly existence (moksha in Vedism, nirvana in Buddhism, and kaivalya in Jainism). As a result, monastic practices mingled with fertility rites. There were confrontations and compromises: Monastic practices such as all-night vigils, fasting, and vegetarianism were adopted by householders; fertility rites such as drawing charms, wearing talismans, building shrines, and making offerings were adopted by monks. Tantra and yoga amalgamated with Vedic, Buddist, and Jain beliefs. Gradually images of buxom, fecund-looking female deities (apsara) and fat, prosperous-looking male deities (yaksha) flanked the idols of the Jain and Buddhist spiritual conquerors known as the Jina and the Buddha. Fertility symbols adorned shrines dedicated to monks. Trees, rocks, rivers, mountains, and animals deemed sacred by the common person became sacred within the Vedic, Buddhist, and Jain folds.

Upon realizing the power of the folk gods and their hold on the minds of people, Vedic brahmanas made a conscious attempt to assimilate these gods into their ideology. This was not difficult; the transition seemed almost natural and effortless. In the age of rituals, the Vedic priest had always felt a power permeating the cosmos when he performed the yagna. In the age of speculation, the Vedic philosopher called this power *Brahman* (meaning "the great") and felt it was present in all things (imminent), yet greater than all things put together (transcendent). In the age of devotion, the Upasana Kanda, the third and final phase of Hinduism, the Vedic theologian personalized the Brahman, giving this lofty idea a form and a name. God came into being.

God, the embodiment of the absolute and ultimate divine principle, was greater than any other god, Vedic or tantric, that existed before. All divinities, spirits, and holy men were projected as mere abbreviations of God. God was the fountainhead of Veda and of dharma and the destination of moksha. Worship of God was equated to yagna and tapasya.

The metamorphosis from elitist Vedic ritualism to populist Hindu theism witnessed the rise of three theistic schools between 400 B.C.E. and A.D. 300, each of which visualized God differently:

- Vaishavism was the worship of Vishnu and his incarnations, mainly Rama and Krishna.
- Shaivism was the worship of Shiva and his sons Murugan and Ganesha.
- Shaktism was the worship of the Goddess, or Devi, as Vishnu's consort Lakshmi, Shiva's consort Gauri, Brahma's consort Saraswati, and her more independent forms, Kali and Durga.

Shiva, Vishnu, and Devi were greater than the Vedic gods. When gods could not defeat demons, God (or Goddess) stepped in.

∽ Kali's Tongue ∽
(Kalika Purana)

Every drop of Raktabija's blood that touched the ground gave rise to another Raktabija. Thus when the gods hurled weapons at this demon, they ended up facing an army of Raktabija clones. Not knowing what to do the gods sought the help of Devi, who transformed into Kali, the dark goddess, and entered the battle-field, naked and with hair unbound, cackling like a hag. She spread her tongue over the earth, preventing Raktabija's blood from touching the ground. Thus no new Raktabija could be created, and he was killed with ease.

Shiva was addressed as Mahadeva, God who is greater than gods, and Ishwara, lord and master. Vishnu was Bhagavan, the all-encompassing being, and Narayana, the refuge of humans. Devi was Shakti, the personification of universal energy, Prakriti, the embodiment of nature, and Maya, the delusion called the world that is constructed by our minds. Maya was mother of all. Stories emerged of how the rishi secured his powers by adoring these manifestations of God.

ᗧ Vishnu Enlightens Brahma ᗧ
(Vishnu Purana)

In the beginning Brahma wondered who he was and from where he came. He looked around and realized he was sitting on a lotus and that its stalk emerged from the navel of a mighty being who reclined on the coils of a great serpent. This being smiled a reassuring smile. He introduced himself as Narayana, the god into whom the universe is absorbed at the end of time. Narayana whispered into Brahma's ear the chants of the Vedas. Thus enlightened, Brahma realized he was to be the father of all beings who reside in the cosmos. He proceeded to do his designated divine duty.

Tales in epics such as the Ramayana and Mahabharata and in chronicles known as the Puranas informed all that devotion to God had more power than any ritual or austerity. In fact, Shiva's wisdom reached humanity not through discourse alone, which appealed only to intellectuals, but also through dance, which was accessible even to the common person (see Fig. 2.9).

⤳ Shiva the Dancer ⤳
(Skanda Purana)

In a forest a group of rishis were performing yagna. A young man entered the forest stark naked. Captivated by his beauty, the wives of the rishis abandoned their rituals and followed him. Their husbands were so angry that they decided to destroy this seducer. While chanting hymns they created a tiger, a serpent, and a goblin out of the sacrificial altar. The youth flayed the tiger alive and wrapped the skin around his waste. He picked up the serpent and wound it around his neck. He then subdued the monster and began dancing on his back. The sages realized this was no ordinary youth. This was Shiva, the Mahadeva. He had through sensual dance overpowered the tiger of desire, the serpent of attachment, and the goblin of forgetfulness. Through him, and not through rituals, they could gain true power—the power to break free from the cycle of rebirths by discovering their true spiritual selves.

The most appealing aspect of theism was that it did not demand renunciation from worldly life. Spiritual rewards were possible within the householder tradition, as long as one diligently performed one's ritually sanctioned role in society, and as long as one adored the absolute divine being. This is expressed in the following narrative. Vyasa, the recompiler of the Veda, is also believed to be the one that put together stories of the Hindu gods. His son Suka, the parrot-headed one, popularized the stories.

⤳ The Return of Vyasa's Son ⤳
(Devi Bhagavata Purana)

Vyasa's son Suka wanted to renounce the world as soon as he was born. He was convinced that women and marriage were the greatest obstacles to release. As Suka walked away from his father's house, Vyasa chased him, recounting the details of

Krishna's life, grace, and beauty. The narrative and the description convinced Suka that to break free from the cycle of rebirths one did not have to abandon worldly life.

Simple rituals were offered as effective alternatives to complex monastic disciplines. One just had to hear the story of Vishnu to acquire every known spiritual merit.

❦ The Death of Parikshit ❦
(Bhagavata Purana)

Parikshit was cursed by a sage to die of a snakebite in seven days. In fear, Parikshit locked himself in a tower. He was haunted by the thought of death, and was advised to hear the story of God. Suka was invited, and he narrated the Bhagavata Purana, the chronicle of Bhagavan. Upon hearing the story Parikshit realized the true meaning of life and overcame his fear of death.

Even chanting the name of a god could garner material and spiritual rewards.

❦ The Power of Rama's Name ❦
(Ramayana)

The brigand Ratnakara justified his misdeeds on the grounds that he had to feed his family. However, when he learned that his wife refused to share the demerits resulting from his misdeeds, he decided to change his ways. He was told by sages to chant the name of Rama. But a life of crime prevented his tongue from articulating the sacred name. So he was asked to chant *mara*, meaning "death," instead. Ratnakara chanted, "Mara, mara, mara . . . ma-ra, ma-ra, ma-ra . . . ra-ma, ra-ma, ra-ma . . . Rama, Rama, Rama." Thus with the passage of time, the word meaning "death" reversed itself to become the name of God. As a result

Ratnakara was purified of all demerits resulting from his misdeeds. He became a saint and a devotee of Rama.

Ritualism did not wane with theism; it transformed. Yagna
was replaced by puja. But while yagna was an end in itself puja
was the means to an end. Yagna compelled gods to do humans'
bidding; through puja humans invoked god, appeased him, and
sought his grace.

Despite the influence of folk rituals, customs, and beliefs on
Buddhism and Jainism, in the mythologies of these religions the
spiritual master—the monk, the Buddha, and the Jina—retained
the primary position. The nastika worldview insisted that the
world was impersonal, that all events were governed by karma,
and that humans alone were responsible for their fate. The gods,
heroes, holy men, and ancestors were as much subject to the laws
of samsara as the rest of the world. Thus in Jain narratives, Rama
and Krishna were not incarnations of Vishnu, who offered liberation from earthly problems; they were mortals as much subject to
earthly laws as the laity. They acquire spiritual rewards not by
participating in worldly life, but by renouncing it.

The Vedic priests offered an alternative view that was more
appealing and empowering. Moreover, one did not have to forsake old practices or old gods in order to worship Vishnu or Shiva.
Folk gods were simply deemed as parochial manifestations of the
cosmic Shiva or Vishnu.

In the southern Indian state of Andhra Pradesh, Mallikarjuna
was a *kshetrapala,* or guardian of the fields, whose consorts were
daughters and goddesses belonging to local communities (see Fig.
2.10). With the rise of theistic Hinduism he came to be seen as a
form of Shiva, and his consorts were seen as forms of Shiva's wife
Parvati. Mythopoesis continues today with Mallikarjuna being
visualized as the transmitter of the grace of the other popular
gods of the region.

Across the length and breadth of India, shrines are associated with stories similar to the one below, which suggests the appropriation of a local shrine within the Brahmanical fold.

∽ The Idol in the Termite Hill ∽
(Temple lore)

A cowherd noticed that his cow emptied its udder over a mysteriously fragrant termite hill. Upon investigation he found inside the hill an idol that the local priest identified as that of Krishna. The image was installed in a temple and adored by devotees.

The new Brahmanical divinities established themselves in villages through stories of courtship and marriage with ancient village goddesses. In the following story Murugan, once a Tamil boy god who was appropriated and assimilated into the Shaiva tradition by being visualized as Shiva's son, becomes the god of a tribal community by marrying one of its daughters.

∽ The Marriage of Valli ∽
(Skanda Purana)

Murugan saw Valli, the tribal maid, in a millet field and fell in love with her. She rebuffed his advances. So he took the help of his brother Vinayaka, who took the form of a mad elephant and chased Valli until she ran straight into Murugan's arms. Murugan shooed the elephant away and won Valli's heart.

In the Puranas, Gods and Goddesses came to be identified with animals, plants, trees, rivers, rocks, and mountains that had always been revered by the masses. For example, the river Ganga had been considered the earthly counterpart of Mandakini (the Milky Way, believed to be the river of gods) since the age of rituals. By the age of devotion, its existence was attributed to Shiva and Vishnu.

ᥫᦉ The Descent of Ganga ᥫᦉ
(Shiva Purana)

Shiva's melodious voice caused Vishnu's feet to melt and transform into a river called Ganga that Brahma contained in a pot.
Years later, at the request of the ascetic Bhagirath, Brahma
agreed to let Ganga descend from the heavens. But the descent
would wash away the earth. To prevent this sage Bhagirath
invoked Shiva, who broke the fall of Ganga by causing her to get
entangled in his matted hair before she landed on earth.

The final blow to Buddhism and Jainism came when the
Buddha and Jina were identified in the Puranas as incarnations of
Vishnu. Common people had always been comfortable with the
idea of deifying revered heroes, mendicants, and ancestors, and
when they found the teachings of the Buddha and the Jina difficult to follow, they chose to deify them instead by placing their
images in shrines, adorning them with flowers, and worshipping
them with fire, water, food, and incense. When it seemed that the
awe-inspiring teacher Buddha was frowning upon people's short-
comings, they turned to a more acceptable divinity: the compassionate Bodhisattva or the maternal Tara, exalted beings who
focused less on liberation and more on helping people out of their
daily tribulations. Vedic brahmanas took advantage of this tendency and went on to project leaders of Buddhism and Jainism as
earthly manifestations of Vishnu, no different from Rama or
Krishna. This made it possible for the commoner to enter the
Vedic fold without abandoning the worship of Buddha or the Jina.
And through convoluted logic the brahmanas even succeeded in
discrediting the teachings of the nastikas by calling them a philosophy taught by God to delude demons.

The Agni Purana informs us that demons followed the Vedic
path and had grown too powerful for the gods to defeat. So the
gods approached Vishnu, who took the form of the Buddha and

the Jina, went to the abode of the asuras, enchanted them with his anti-Vedic teachings, and made them give up mantras, yagnas, and tapas until they became so powerless that they were defeated with great ease (see Fig. 2.11).

As Buddhism waned from the spiritual landscape of India by the eighth century, most people were convinced that the answer to all of life's problems lay in adoration of God. With time a question arose: Which god?

Many deities vied for the position of the highest god, the true and total embodiment of the ultimate divine principle. The foremost contenders were Shiva and Vishnu. The resulting rivalry between the Shaivas and Vaishnavas gave rise to narratives that tried to establish the superiority of one god over another.

ᴄᴏ The Pillar of Fire ᴄᴏ
(Shiva Purana)

Both Brahma and Vishnu claimed the title of Mahadeva, the greatest of gods. Suddenly there appeared between them a fiery pillar that seemed to have neither a beginning nor an end. Vishnu took the form of a boar and tried to find the pillar's base, but failed. Brahma took the form of a swan and tried to find its top, but failed. From within the fiery pillar emerged Shiva. Brahma and Vishnu acknowledged him as the greatest of gods.

Just as this story projects Shiva to be greater than Vishnu, the following story projects Vishnu as being greater than Shiva.

ᴄᴏ Mohini to the Rescue ᴄᴏ
(Vishnu Purana)

Shiva once gave an asura the power to burn anyone with the touch of his hand. The ingrate tried to touch Shiva himself. Upon realizing his mistake, Shiva ran and sought the help of Vishnu, who took the form of the damsel Mohini and distracted the asura. The asura was captivated by Mohini's beauty and asked her to marry him. "Only if you dance just like I do," said Mohini. The asura agreed and followed Mohini's movements. At the climax of the dance Mohini touched her head. The asura did the same and was reduced to ashes. In gratitude Shiva saluted Vishnu.

Sometimes the confrontation between different theistic schools turned violent. Intermarriage between Vaishanvas and Shaivas ceased. Both groups tried to lay claim to as many folk gods as they could. This was not always possible. Both Shaivas and Vaishnavas claimed Ayyappa, a tribal god in Kerala (see Fig. 2.12). A compromise was reached through narrative that declared him the son of both Shiva and Vishnu.

༝ The Birth of Ayyappa ༝
(Sabarimalai Sthala Purana)

When Shiva saw Vishnu in the form of the enchantress Mohini he was so excited that he shed his semen. The child thus born was called Hari-Hara-Suta, the son of Vishnu and Shiva. He was given to the care of a childless king in Kerala. When Hari-Hara-Suta grew up he defended the land against demons but refused any material rewards. Everyone realized this ascetic warrior was a manifestation of God.

As theism became part of the mainstream kings began to patronize it. The Gupta period (circa 300) saw the gradual rise of temple tradition. Not satisfied with approaching the divine through trees, animals, rivers, and natural rock formations, the kings sponsored the making of idols of Gods and Goddesses in metal and stone that were enshrined in temples. Between 800 and 1300 vast temple complexes came into being. These were controlled and managed by brahmanas, who once again came to dominate society. As in the age of rituals, in the age of devotion they became the conduits of divinity, patronized by kings and the newly emerging landed gentry.

Caste hierarchy manifested in the temple tradition too with *jati* (caste based on occupation) determining whether one was allowed to enter the temple or not. With rituals came the idea of pollution. Those at the bottom of the caste hierarchy—sweepers, cobblers, and other menial laborers—were the most polluted.

Just as the rise of ascetics challenged ritualism in the pre-Christian era, the bhakti movement challenged the temple culture. *Bhakti* means "unconditional surrender to the will of God," without the intervention of any priest or ritual. The idea of direct communion with a personal god while rejecting all caste constraints first emerged in the passionate songs of Tamil poet-saints known as Alvars and Nayanars in the early centuries of the common era. The idea of direct communion, which was most likely of non-Vedic origin, was incorporated into the Vedic fold when scholars like Shakara, Ramanuja, Madhava, Nimbarka, Chaitanya, and Vallabha used Vedanta as the underlying principle of bhakti. Stories such as the following popularized the idea of real over ritual adoration of the divine.

∾ God Turns for Kanaka Dasa ∾
(Udipi Sthala Purana)

The shepherd Kanaka was not allowed to enter the temple of Krishna at Udipi because of his low caste. He wandered around the temple with tears in his eyes and burst into a passionate song, appealing to the presiding deity to show himself. Suddenly the image in the sanctum sanctorum turned around, and through a crack that appeared in the temple wall the shepherd devotee was able to see the lord.

Emotion mattered more than mere expression. God demanded true affection, not ritual adoration. God paid no attention to artificial constructs such as caste or gender.

⚬ The Hunter's Eye ⚬
(Periyar Purana)

Both a priest and a hunter worshipped Shiva. The priest followed rites prescribed by the Agamas in his worship. The hunter knew no rituals but always offered Shiva a portion of his hunt. To test who was a greater devotee, two real eyes appeared on the image of Shiva. They began to bleed. The priest ran away, taking this to be a bad omen. The hunter, however, gouged out his eyes to replace the bleeding eyes of Shiva. This real gesture of love mattered more to Shiva than ritual worship. Pleased, Shiva showered blessings on the hunter.

The arrival of Islam around 1000, with its uncompromising stance against idolatory and the caste system and its absolute submission to the idea of the Divine, had a powerful impact on the bhakti movement. It fueled the Sant tradition that preferred to visualize the Divine without form and without the intervention of a mediator. Everyone had direct access to God, irrespective of caste or gender.

INVASIONS AND IMMIGRATIONS

India has had its share of invaders and immigrants. First were the Persians (circa 400 B.C.E.), and then the Greeks (circa 300 B.C.E), followed by hordes of Central Asian tribes such as the Kushans, Sakas, Pallavas, Huns, and Gujars (circa 200 B.C.E. to A.D. 400). Then came the Islamic invasion (circa 1000) that established the Delhi sultanate and Moghul empire in the north and the Bahmani empire and Shahi kingdom in the south. Finally, the European colonial powers arrived in India (circa 1500).

Many, like the Rajputs, whose roots have been traced to the Scythians (Sakas) and Gujars, assimilated themselves with the Hindus by tracing their origins to mythical kings like Rama. Others resisted assimilation or introduced new thoughts to the Hindu worldview. The most important of these was the idea of evil. The Manichaean idea that the cosmos is the battlefield of divine and evil forces has its origin in ancient Persia, where all good in the world was ascribed to Ahura Mazda while all bad was ascribed to the evil Angra Manyu. When these ideas came to India the cosmic architecture changed. Until then the celestial realms were the abode of the devas, the subterranean realms were the abode of the asuras, and the devas and asuras were just different beings populating the cosmos and fighting over cosmic bounty, or Shri. The Manichaean influence transformed the battle of the devas and the asuras into a moral conflict. Devas became the sacred forces of dharma, or order; asuras became evil forces of adharma, or anarchy. Vishnu-loka, the abode of Vishnu, and Shiva-loka, the abode of Shiva, were equated with the biblical heaven, where the good would reside forever instead of being reborn. Naraka, a subterranean realm, came into being; it was equated with the biblical hell, where wrongdoers would be punished. Yama, the god who presides over death and rebirth, became the great moral judge.

ᘓ The Death of the Pandavas ᘓ
(Mahabharata)

When Yudhishtira, the eldest Pandava, reached Swarga, the abode of Indra, he did not find his brothers there. Instead he found the Kauravas, the villains who had provoked a war that had led to the death of millions. "How can this be?" he asked Indra, king of the devas. Indra informed him that the Kauravas had died on the battlefield upholding their duty as warriors, and hence were transported to heaven. Indra then led Yudhishtira to a dark and miserable place under the earth where amid the sounds of pain and torture he found his brothers. Bhima was suffering because of his gluttony, Arjuna for his pride over being the greatest archer, Nakula for being vain about his beauty, and Sahadeva for being haughty about his intelligence.

Another major influence was the idea of a messiah who would come down and restore the world to its former glory. This idea probably reached India through followers of Zoroaster who migrated to India from Persia, or through Muslim and Christian migrants and traders. It gave hope to millions of Hindus who faced persecution following the establishment of Muslim kingdoms in India.

In support of the idea of a messiah, the Bhavishya Purana says that when dharma on Earth is totally abandoned and the ensuing disorder becomes unbearable, Vishnu will descend as a warrior called Kalki on a white horse, sword in hand (see Fig. 2.13). He will kill all wrongdoers, anarchists, and unrighteous people and then reestablish dharma.

The idea of a god who restores the world to its former glory does not quite fit in with the cyclical view of life in Hinduism. Hindus had in Vishnu a god who restores order. As Rama and Krishna he prevents the world from dying an untimely death, but he does not halt the march of time. Vishnu walks the earth as Krishna in a later age than Rama; the world he faces is more corrupt than the one in which Rama lived. Although Rama restores dharma on earth before returning to his heavenly abode, he does not arrest the natural degeneration of the cosmos as determined by time. In the Kalki story, however, Vishnu not only prevents the untimely death of the world, he also restores youth. The idea is reminiscent of the resurrection and the second coming: Christ helps in regaining paradise, though the return is informed by slavery in Egypt, exile to Babylon, and persecution by Rome.

That the overthrow of barbarians and foreigners was equated with the establishment of order indicates the level of hostility felt by Hindus toward their Muslim rulers. To make peace between otherwise antagonistic Muslims and Hindus in South India, stories emerged in which Muslim warriors became comrades of Hindu gods. These helped bridge the communal gap.

∽ Manikantha and Vavar ∽ (Sabarimalai Sthala Purana)

Manikantha [an alternate name for Ayyappa], the son of Shiva and Vishnu, went about the world killing demons. In all Manikantha's missions Vavar, a Muslim warrior, accompanied him. As he was pleased with Vavar's loyalty and his strength in battle, Manikantha declared that he would not accept any prayers in his temple until his devotees paid obeisance at the *dargah*, or burial site, of Vavar.

In the great temple complexes of South India, Muslim princesses were enshrined as devotees whose devotion to the presiding deity had transformed them into consorts.

∽ Ranganatha's Muslim Bride ∽ (Shrirangam Sthala Purana)

With great difficulty the saint Ramanuja managed to bring back the sacred idol of Ranganatha, the presiding deity of Shrirangam that had been taken to Delhi by a Muslim warlord. The warlord's daughter had become so fond of the idol that she followed Ramanuja to Shrirangam and died on the doorsteps of the temple while seeking a glimpse of her beloved. She has since been revered as Manavala Mamunigal, the divine consort of Ranganatha. Her painting has been put in a temple located within the sacred complex.

Saint Thomas is believed to have brought Christianity to India almost around the same time that it reached Rome. The influence of Christianity has been observed in some Indian philosophies. Madhava, the thirteenth-century philosopher, did not agree with the Vedic idea that the soul of all sentient beings, *jiva-atma,* is in essence the same as that of God, *param-atma.* He differentiated between the creator, who he visualized as Vishnu, and creation. According to the mythosphere Madhava established, only Vayu, the wind god, visualized as Hanuman, who was the son of Vishnu, could establish the connection between jiva-atma and param-atma. Madhava also believed in the doctrine of eternal damnation. Most beings go through cycles of life and death, but some—those who cross the line—end up in hell and have no hope of being reborn or released unless they appeal to Vayu. Christian missionaries who arrived in India after Vasco da Gama discovered the sea route to India in the fifteenth century and were amazed by the similarities between the tale of Krishna, the cowherd, and Jesus, the shepherd. They did not rule out the possibility of a Christian influence in this Hindu tradition.

CONCLUSION

Hindu narratives have been edited, symbols have been reinterpreted, and rituals have evolved over the centuries as the Hindus fought, fled, and froze to cope with the vagaries of nature and culture. As a result Hinduism today is quite different from the Hinduism practiced four thousand years ago. Still, symbols dated to 2000 B.C.E. embellish contemporary Hindu temples, hymns composed around 1500 B.C.E. are chanted even today, and philosophies codified around 500 B.C.E. still guide Hindus in times of crisis.

Narratives themselves have not remained static with time or space. Some narratives that existed as fragments in earlier texts became full bodied in later texts and even came to possess a number of versions—the transformations effected by sociocultural changes and the needs of the people. The following table shows how the story of the sacred boar has transformed with time (see Table 26).

For a good example of how narratives and symbols transform with space we observe how the gods Ganesha and Kartikeya are treated in different parts of India. Both are sons of Shiva. Ganesha is an intelligent elephant-headed and potbellied scribe of the sages while Kartikeya is a sharp, lean, and tough warlord of the

TABLE 26. TRANSFORMATION OF A NARRATIVE OVER TIME

Period	Narrative
Verses used during the yagna ceremony (circa 800 B.C.E.)	In the form of the boar Emusha, Prajapati scooped up earth with his tusks from the bottom of the sea and spread it on a lotus leaf to create the earth (Brahmanas).
Rise of Vishnu as the focus of devotion, acquiring the characteristics of earlier Vedic gods such as Prajapati, who waned in significance (circa 500 B.C.E.)	The demon Hiranyaksha dragged the earth goddess Bhudevi under the sea. Hearing her cries, Vishnu emerged from Brahma's nostril in the form of a boar, plunged into the sea, gored the demon to death, placed Bhudevi on his snout, and raised her to the surface (Vishnu Purana).
Rise of Krishna as the greatest incarnation of Vishnu, greater than any Vedic god	The union of Varaha and Bhudevi under the sea resulted in the birth of the demon Naraka, who terrorized the devas until Krishna came to their rescue and killed Naraka (Bhagavata Purana).
Rivalry between devotees of Shiva and Vishnu (circa A.D. 1300)	United with Bhudevi, Varaha lost all interest in returning to Vaikuntha as Vishnu. The sons he fathered terrorized the three worlds. Furious, Shiva took the form of a bull, gored Varaha's sons to death, flayed Varaha alive with his horns and liberated Vishnu from the delusion of earthly life (Shiva Purana).

TABLE 27. DIFFERENT PHASES OF HINDUISM AS PRESENTED IN THE
RAMAYANA

Phase of Hinduism	Narrative in Ramayana
Vedic ritualism	Dasharatha gets sons by performing a yagna
Post-Vedic asceticism	Ravana and his brothers obtain the favor of Brahma through acts of self-denial and austerity
Brahmanical ideology	Dasharatha plans to crown Rama king and retire to the forest; Sita has to undergo a trial of fire to prove she has been chaste even in captivity; Rama has to undergo expiation for the sin of killing Ravana, because although he is a villain he is by caste a brahmana
Bhakti philosophy	Hanuman, who serves Rama selflessly, becomes the embodiment of devotion and an object of worship

gods. In North India, Ganesha is the younger brother who is married while Kartikeya is the older brother who is unmarried. In South India, Ganesha is the older brother who is single while Kartikeya is the younger brother with two wives.

The innumerous transformations have been organic enough to offer a sense of continuity. New ideas did not replace old ones; they were assimilated to generate better ideas. The best example of this is the epic Ramayana. As the narrative unfolds there are references to Vedic ritualism, post-Vedic asceticism, Upanishadic speculation, Brahmanical ideology, and bhakti philosophy, without any sense of conflict or contradiction (see Table 27).

❖ 4 ❖
Mythography:
Interpreting Myth

$\mathcal{M}$yths may not satisfy the demands of rationality or science, but they contain profound wisdom—provided one believes they do and is willing to find out what they communicate. That is precisely the purpose of mythography.

A lot depends on the intention of interpretation. Broadly, all schools of mythography can be classified into two groups:

- Those that believe one can outgrow myths by discovering the truth
- Those that believe that all truths are constructed by myths

In the former myth is reduced to history, allegory, or pseudo- or primitive science, and is seen as a medium for or a flawed version of an immutable, eternal reality created by or for unsophisticated minds. In the second school mythmaking is an essential function of the mind (conscious or unconscious) to express repressed needs and desires or to make sense out of life and resolve all conflicts therein.

In this chapter we shall discover the different ways a myth can be interpreted, focusing primarily on the historical, strategic, allegorical, and psychological.

HISTORY AND PREHISTORY

Many people are convinced that at the heart of an epic or legend is an event that occurred a long time ago, that narratives become sacred because they are the only available records (however distorted and embellished they may be) of a community's past. To these people the Trojan war did occur, Moses did lead the Hebrews across the Red Sea to Palestine, Arthur was once an ancient Celtic king, and Osiris was a wise Egyptian leader and harbinger of civilization whose murder at the hands of the boorish Set was avenged by his brave son, Horus.

The idea that myth is nothing but warped or hyperbolic history goes back to 300 B.C.E., when the Greek philosopher Euhemerus of Messene wrote in his *Sacred Documents* that Zeus and other gods of Olympus were in fact deified humans. In India medieval Jain scholars, in their commentaries on the Hindu epic Ramayana, opined that the monkeys of the narrative were in reality tribes whose banners bore the emblem of monkeys.

Hindu scriptures rarely differentiate between traditional beliefs and historical data. Hence the oldest collections of myths are known as Itihasas (histories) and Puranas (chronicles). In these documents narratives of gods, kings, and sages trace the history of India from the beginning of time to the prophecies of anarchy that will herald the end of the world. Historians, however, do not consider these narratives to be records of facts.

Early Indian history is shrouded in mystery. First there were the stark, functional, brick-laden cities built along the tributaries of the Indus and the now-dry Saraswati around 2500 B.C.E. About the same time the earliest Vedic hymns were being composed. This civilization, covering a territory of more than 1.3 million square kilometers, disappeared around 1500 B.C.E. as inexplicably as it appeared. Some believe that the composers of the Vedic hymns destroyed the civilization; others believe the cities simply died out, letting Vedic culture dominate society. Still others believe that the Vedic culture was spawned within and around the city civilization itself. For more than a thousand years, from the collapse of the city civilization to the establishment of the Magadhan empire following Alexander's invasion, historians have no material relics for the study of Indian history. There are no ruins of cities, no monuments or inscriptions. The only archaeological evidence for this vast stretch of time are a few tools and potsherds. In place of material evidence there is Vedic literature, which is primarily liturgical and philosophical but which offers tantalizing glimpses of the historical conditions that witnessed the spread of Vedic culture from northwest India to the east, and then south of the subcontinent. Given this situation historians, anthropologists, and sociologists often turn to the tales of the Itihasas and Puranas to understand what could have happened in India between 1500 B.C.E. and A.D. 500.

Hindu narratives clearly retain the memory of the integration of three main groups of people whose ideas fermented the Hindu psyche: nomadic herdsmen, settled agriculturists, and animist hunter-gatherers of the forest. If one believes that myth is essentially protohistory then the following story clearly refers to a war involving the nomadic herdsmen, the agriculturists, and forest tribes.

⤬ The Sons of Kadru and Vinata ⤬
(Mahabharata)

Kadru, the mother of serpents, or nagas, and Vinata, the mother of the eagle known as Garuda, once saw the celestial horse

Ucchaishrava gliding along the horizon at dawn. Kadru said the horse had black hair in its tail; Vinata said the horse was spotlessly white and wagered her freedom on it. Determined to win the wager, Kadru ordered her children to cling to the horse's tail. The next day, from a distance Ucchaishrava's tail did appear to have black hair. As a result Vinata had no choice but to serve as Kadru's slave.

The price of Vinata's freedom was the jar of amrita, the nectar of immortality that was possessed by the devas. Garuda flew into the city of Amravati, fought the devas, took the jar of amrita by force, and gave it to the nagas, thus securing his mother's freedom. He requested that the nagas drink the amrita only after taking a bath. While they were away he let Indra, king of the devas, reclaim the nectar and take it back to his celestial city. Thus Garuda tricked the nagas, just as their mother had tricked his mother. Impressed by Garuda's strength, valor, and guile, Vishnu—the best of gods—asked Garuda to be his mount. "I will carry you around if you can place me on top of you too." Vishnu agreed, and Garuda became both his mount and his insignia (fluttering on his banner above him). On Garuda's request Vishnu also made the nagas the natural food of eagles so that each time Garuda killed a naga he did not sin.

Even today in Vishnu temples the image of Garuda holding a serpent in his talons can be seen before the sanctum sanctorum and on the sacred banner. The above narrative, which explains the origin of this practice, can also be interpreted as a historical event: The serpent-worshipping agriculturists had enslaved the eagle-totem tribe and stolen cows (indicated by amrita, since cows were crucial to the survival of the nomads) belonging to the nomads. The leader of the eagle tribe befriended the nomads, and together they liberated the cows as well as the slaves.

South Indian folklore, especially from Kerala, retains the memory of the migration of the nagas from the north, where their forest homes were destroyed by migrating aryas. There are tales and ceremonies referring to the only survivor, the serpent-king Takshaka, who in exchange for shelter ensured the fertility of the land. It is likely that the nagas were serpent-worshipping agriculturists, who after being driven south by animal-herding aryas taught farming to the southern forest dwellers who gave them refuge. In time the identity of the fertility-bestowing serpents and the people who first worshipped them mingled and merged. The teacher of farming who worshipped the naga became a naga himself.

The Bhagavata Purana informs us that Kaliya, the naga, and his wives took shelter in a lake to hide from the eagle Garuda, who wanted to kill and eat them. This lake stood near Gokul, the village of the cowherds. To keep away trespassers Kaliya poisoned the lake with his venom and attacked anyone who dared to enter the water. Krishna, the cowherd hero, challenged Kaliya to a fight. He ended up subduing the naga and dancing on his hood until his wives begged for his release (see Fig. 2.14). The story suggests that agriculturists (represented by Kaliya) harassed by forest tribes (represented by Garuda) migrated to pastures where herdsmen (represented by Krishna) grazed their cows. After a period of hostility, the herdsmen overpowered the agriculturists, befriended them, and finally gave them protection.

Some historians believe that such narratives came into being when certain Indo-European nomads (yagna-performing, cow-herding aryas, mythologically identified as gods and humans, or devas and manavas) made their way into India from the northwest. They invaded settled communities (of serpent-worshipping, city-building dravidas, mythologically identified as asuras, yakshas, rakshasas, and nagas), which had driven out autochthonous tribal cultures (totemic and animistic communities, mythologically identified as vanaras, garudas, bhalukas, and nishadhas).

These historians believe that the aryas brought horses to India and that in a ceremony known as Ashwameda they let loose their most magnificent horse and laid claim to all the lands the horse traversed unchallenged. Stories such as the one below seem to endorse this idea.

∽ Yudhishtira's Horse Sacrifice ∽ (Mahabharata)

When the Pandava Yudhishtira became king, he performed a horse sacrifice and let loose his royal horse. Arjuna led the armies that followed this horse. The horse crossed many lands and the kings of those lands accepted the overlordship of the Pandavas. But then on the border of Manipura, the warrior Babruvahana stopped the stallion and challenged Arjuna to a duel. In the fight that followed Babruvahana successfully shot a poison-tipped arrow into Arjuna's chest. When Babruvahana's mother, Chitrangada, saw the dying Arjuna she burst into tears, for Arjuna was her husband—Babruvahana's father—who as per the marriage contract had agreed to let her father, who had no male offspring, adopt the son born of their union. Babruvahana had never seen his father. He had learned archery from Uloopi, a naga woman who was also Arjuna's wife, but one he had forgotten soon after marriage. Thus scorned, she had used Babruvahana to avenge her humiliation. At the request of Babruvahana and Chitrangada, Uloopi brought Arjuna back to life with the help of the serpent gem that serves as an antidote against all poisons.

Anthropologists suggest that Chitrangada probably belonged to a matrilineal clan—not unlike the Nairs of Kerala—where the child belongs to the mother's, not the father's, family. The arrival of Vedic culture is believed to have replaced an earlier matriarchal culture with a patriarchal one.

The Aryan invasion theory, based primarily on linguistic studies of the Vedic scriptures, is fraught with contradictions and controversies, for it suggests that the Vedic culture came into India from outside, an idea that is unacceptable to the traditional Hindu of modern India. While narratives suggest a constant dynamic of conflict and compromise between nomads, settled communities, and the forest tribes, they never suggest that the nomads (whether Rama or Yayati or the Pandavas) are outsiders. Also the scriptures insist that the three groups of people descended from a common father—Kashyapa, the ancient one— indicating a common ancestry. This is seen as proof of the alternative to the Aryan invasion theory: that the Vedic culture once extended from India to the Caspian Sea (*Caspian* being a derivative or corruption of *Kashyapa,* which is the name of the rishi who fathered the gods) but survived and evolved only in the subcontinent. Indeed many of the characters in the epics Ramayana and Mahabharata (Kaikeyi, stepmother of Rama; Madri, wife of Pandu; Gandhari, wife of Dhritarashtra) belong to lands now identified as Pakistan and Afghanistan (see Table 28).

When the story of Krishna is analyzed from a historical angle, it seems that Krishna, the God, emerged from the union of two heroes: one rural and one urban. The story of Krishna's early life is very pastoral. He is associated with animal husbandry, while his brother Balarama, always depicted with a plough, is associated with agriculture.

᧰ Krishna's Early Life ᧰
(Harivamsa)

Krishna was raised in the village of cowherds. As a child he raided dairies for butter, played pranks on milkmaids, and won the hearts of all with his endearing mischief. As a youth his winsome smile charmed the women. Enchanted by the music of his flute, the women would slip out of their houses on moonlit nights to dance and sing with Krishna on the banks of Yamuna. During the day he took care of the cows. He protected the village from many demons who sought entry by taking the shape of a horse, a python, a stork, a calf, and even a cowherd. Krishna also saved the village from a whirlwind by choking it with his bare hands, from a forest fire by swallowing the flames, and from torrential rain by picking up a mountain with his little finger so that it served as an umbrella sheltering the entire community.

The king of Mathura, Kamsa, feared Krishna's strength and popularity and invited him to the city to participate in a wrestling match. Krishna defeated all the wrestlers, and instead of being killed in the arena ended up killing the king of Mathura, who was hated by all. It was then revealed that Krishna was no ordinary cowherd but, in fact, the nephew of Kamsa raised incognito, as it had been foretold that he would be the killer of his uncle.

TABLE 28. THREE GROUPS OF PEOPLE WHOSE WORLDVIEWS FORM THE HINDU PARADIGM

	Nomad	Settled Community	Forest Dweller
ECONOMIC ACTIVITY	Animal husbandry	Agriculture and mining	Hunting and gathering
HISTORICAL IDENTITY	Arya	Dravida	Nishadha
MYTHOLOGICAL IDENTITY	Deva, manava	Asura, naga, rakshasa, yaksha	Vanara, garuda
PHILOSOPHY	Vedic speculation on the delusory nature of the world and its truth hidden in Vedic scriptures and rituals	Tantric speculation on the world being a manifestation of energy that can be manipulated with prayer and penance	Attributing consciousness to every element in the plant, animal, and mineral worlds
RITUAL	Yagna	Puja, vrata	Trance, possession

While in his early life he was a prince among cowherds, in later life he was a cowherd among princes.

∽ Krishna's Later Life ∽
(Mahabharata)

News of Kamsa's death angered Jarasandha, king of Magadha, who was Kamsa's father-in-law. Jarasandha attacked Mathura seventeen times. Each time Krishna repelled the attack. When Jarasandha attacked once again Krishna realized it was prudent for his people, the Yadavas, to move to a safer location. They moved to the island of Dwaraka in the western sea.

Krishna then befriended the Pandavas, his cousins who belonged to the Kuru clan. Krishna helped the Pandavas inherit their share of their kingdom and build a very prosperous city called Indraprastha. With their help, Krishna had Jarasandha killed. Unfortunately, the Pandavas gambled away their kingdom for thirteen years to their cousins the Kauravas. At the end of this period the Kauravas refused to return the kingdom. Krishna tried in vain to negotiate peace. When it failed he helped the Pandavas wage war against their cousins.

What followed was a bloody war on the plains of Kurukshetra in which the Pandavas triumphed. Years later, differences over who was more righteous—the Pandavas or the Kauravas—led to a civil war among the Yadavas in which Krishna witnessed the death of all his kinsmen. Krishna was killed accidentally by a hunter while resting in the forest. The sea rose to submerge his city. The women who survived were raped and abducted by barbarians. A few Yadavas survived and were given shelter by the Pandavas.

There is a stark contrast between the two halves of Krishna's life, suggesting that there is a forced amalgamation of two biographies and the transformation of the amalgamated hero into a manifestation of God.

Sometimes the historical school of myth includes some rather uncomfortable details. The following story, for example, suggests that human sacrifice was probably not unknown in the Vedic culture.

ᶜ᷉ The Sacrifice of Sunahshepas ᷉ᶜ
(Mahabharata)

King Harishchandra wanted a son so desperately that he promised Varuna, the sea god, that if he could only became a father he would sacrifice his son in the sixteenth year of his life. The son was born, and sixteen years passed, but Harishchandra could not bring himself to sacrifice the boy. Infuriated, Varuna struck Harishchandra with dropsy. The king begged for mercy and a compromise was reached. Varuna agreed to the sacrifice of any sixteen-year-old brahmana boy. Only one brahmana agreed to part with his son, Sunahshepas, but only in exchange for a hundred cows.

The lad was brought to the sacrificial altar. When Vishwamitra, the presiding priest, realized that the sacrificial beast was a human he was horrified. He taught the boy a hymn to appease Varuna and escape this fate. At the appointed hour no priest was willing to tie the boy to the sacrificial post. Again the boy's father agreed to do the needful for a price. Then it was time to behead the boy. Again the boy's father agreed to do so for a price. Sunahshepas wept but no one heard his cry, so he began chanting the hymn to Varuna. So melodious was his voice that the devas descended from the celestial regions and stopped the sacrifice. Vishwamitra was made the foster father of the boy, who was blessed by Indra. The gods declared they would never again accept human sacrifice.

The following story refers to the once common practice of *levirate,* asking the wife of a man who is either dead or impotent to cohabit with another man to bear children.

∾ The Children of Vichitravirya ∾
(Mahabharata)

Vichitravirya died, leaving behind two childless widows: Ambika and Ambalika. So Vichitravirya's mother, Satyavati, called the sage Vyasa to do the needful. He went to Ambika, who shut her eyes while they made love; as a result she bore a blind son called Dhirtarashtra. Vyasa then went to Ambalika, who turned pale when she saw his austere visage. Pandu, the child she bore, was pale and sickly. Satyavati asked Vyasa to stay and father a health-ier child. This time the two widows did not oblige, instead send-ing their maid, who made love without any fear or disgust. She bore a perfect son called Vidura. When Satyavati learned that the widows had sent a maid in their place she was angry. She tried to force the widows, but Vyasa told her to stop. "Such things are not to be done by force," he said.

Stories such as the one below even suggest that sex-hospitality, the practice of a wife offering sexual favors to a guest with the blessings of her husband, was not unknown in ancient India.

∾ Oghavati's Obedience ∾
(Mahabharata)

Sudarshana had asked his wife, Oghavati, to please his guests in every way. While he was away a mendicant arrived at their doorstep. Instead of alms he asked for a sexual favor, and Oghavati obliged. While the two were having intercourse Sudarshana returned. He called out to his wife and she said, "I am busy satisfying the desire of our guest." Sudarshana replied, "Carry on. I will wait till you are done." The mendicant turned out to be Dharma, lord of righteous conduct. He was pleased with the couple and blessed them for upholding the social law.

Closely linked to the historical school of myth is the fascinating antediluvian school. This school believes that myths, though distorted, are the only records of real events that occurred in the distant past. But this past is not quite the past of historians. In the antediluvian school, the past is a time at least fifteen thousand years ago, sometimes even more, before the Ice Age, when a highly evolved civilization spread across the globe via a sophisticated understanding of mathematics, astronomy, architecture, and telepathy.

This school is sometimes called the Atlantis school. It rejects what traditional history has to say about prehistory—that after the Ice Age humans moved from being cave-dwelling hunter-gatherers to settled agriculturists or nomadic herdsmen, and then to city dwellers, empire builders, and finally scientists. It postulates that the Ice Age marks the end of a great civilization known to the Greeks as Atlantis. When scriptures talk of a Golden Age they refer not to an imagined utopia but a real period in human history whose memory remains only in myth. The people of this civilization were mathematicians, and hence scientists. They applied their knowledge to the stars, to buildings, and to technology to create a highly evolved culture. They knew how to harness the forces of nature using telepathy, crystals, and sound. The exact science is forgotten but remnants remain in astrology, numerology, and geomancy. In present times these subjects are deemed "occult"; most people do not realize that these subjects were once "sciences."

In Hindu scriptures, there is repeated mention of rishis who knew the secrets of the Veda and who transmitted it orally to worthy students. The antediluvian school believes the rishis were the keepers of Atlantian wisdom. Stories such as the following have caused many to speculate that ancient Hindu rishis knew the art of in vitro fertilization.

◠ Gandhari's Children ◠
(Mahabharata)

The sage Vyasa had blessed Gandhari that she would bear a hundred sons. Unfortunately, Gandhari gave birth to a ball of flesh, as hard and cold as metal, after two years of pregnancy. Distraught, she approached Vyasa, who asked Gandhari to cut the ball of flesh into a hundred pieces and place each piece in a jar of clarified butter. Vyasa then chanted hymns and blessed the pots. Nine months later the pots were broken. In each pot there was a male child. Thus the hundred sons of Gandhari, the Kauravas, were born.

The following story from the Mahabharata is taken as evidence that the ancients knew ballistic and probably even nuclear technology.

◠ Krishna Curses Ashwathama ◠
(Mahabharata)

The war was over. The Pandavas had won, having killed all the Kauravas. Only three warriors in the enemy army had survived. One of them was Ashwathama. Determined to avenge the Kaurava defeat he raised his bow, chanted a dreaded formula, transformed his arrow into the Brahmastra missile, and let it go. Arjuna, the Pandava archer, saw the missile approach and let loose a similar missile to counter Ashwathama's attack. "Stop," cried Vyasa, grandfather of the Pandavas and Kauravas and author of the Mahabharata epic. "Reverse the formula, recall the missile; otherwise the collision will destroy all life. The world will crumble, forests will burn, seas will dry up, and nothing will remain." Arjuna did as he was advised. Ashwathama did not know how to recall his missile so he directed it toward the womb of Uttara to kill her unborn child. Krishna came to the rescue of the fetus: He entered Uttara's womb, countered the missile, saved the unborn child, came out, and cursed the dastardly Ashwathama that he would live forever, his body covered with sores and ulcers that would never heal.

The science-fiction school is an offshoot of the antediluvian school. Here the wisdom of Atlantis is perceived as a gift of extraterrestrial beings who visited earth on spaceships. Followers of this school believe that only this extraordinary event can explain the existence of grand and mysterious structures like the pyramids of Egypt and South America, earth images on the Nazca plateau in the Andes that can only be seen aerially, the Serpent Mound in North America, and Stonehenge in England. To these believers tales of cities in the sky are not fantasy but ancient records of spaceships. The following story is thus viewed as a great war between missile-shooting Atlantians and spaceship-riding extraterrestrials.

⧸⧸ Shiva Destroys Tripura ⧸⧸
(Linga Purana)

Three asuras secured the boon to build three aerial cities that could only be destroyed by a single arrow. When these cities of gold, silver, and iron were built the asuras roamed across every plane of existence, causing mayhem wherever they went. The devas went to Shiva, who said that the asuras were invulnerable until they respected the Veda. So Vishnu entered the city as the wily sage Mayamoha Buddha and deluded them with his logic until they abandoned the Veda. Then Shiva prepared himself, for the earth was his chariot, the sun and moon served as its wheels, the Veda were its horses, and Brahma was its charioteer (see Fig. 2.15). Mount Meru was his bow, Ananta Sesha was his bowstring, and Vishnu himself was his arrow.

Shiva chased the cities for a thousand years, waiting for them to align themselves in a single line. This happened for just a moment, and Shiva fired a missile that ripped through the three cities and destroyed them in an instant. The cries of the asuras filled the three worlds as the aerial cities tumbled down. Shiva wept when he heard their cry, for the asuras were his devotees. Such was his wailing, more heart wrenching than his war cry, that he came to be known as Rudra, the howler. From his tears came the Rudraksha beads that are sacred to every devotee of Shiva. Shiva also smeared his forehead with three horizontal lines of ash to remind all of this terrible event.

The Ramayana talks about a flying chariot called *pushpaka-vimana* (see Fig. 2.16). To many the account of this chariot is not poetic imagination but historical evidence that airplanes existed in Vedic times. The chariot belonged to the yaksha-king Kubera. Ravana took it by force after driving Kubera out of Lanka. Ravana used the chariot to abduct Sita. After killing Ravana and rescuing Sita, Rama returned to the city of Ayodhya on this flying chariot.

STRATEGIC CHARTERS

Narratives are often strategic, aimed at making a people think a particular way. They can help establish hierarchy in society, define relationships between men and women, or attribute sacredness to a shrine. These narratives are not unconscious outpourings of the psyche; they are deliberate attempts to impose an ideology. They transform artificial constructions into natural phenomena.

According to the Vedic ideology of varna-ashrama-dharma, members of a society had to function according to duties (dharma) that are determined by their station in society, which is determined by birth (varna) and their stage in life (ashrama). Those who did not agree with this ideology were barbarians, and it was divinely ordained that they must be driven away.

☙ The Churning of Vena's Corpse ❧
(Bhagavata Purana)

King Vena did not respect the varna-ashrama-dharma. Angry, the earth goddess refused to bear fruit. When the sages realized what was happening they picked up blades of grass that turned into weapons and killed Vena. The sages then churned his dead body. The polluting elements were cast away. This substance turned into a nasty-looking creature that was driven into the forest. The creature was the forefather of the nishadhas, or forest tribes.

From the pure remnants the sages created the perfect king, Prithu, who was given the bow of sovereignty by the gods. Prithu asked the earth to release her wealth. She refused and ran away in the form of a cow. Prithu chased her, raised his bow, subdued her with the threat to shoot her, and finally reassured her that he would uphold dharma. He then led all living beings to milk her by the code of dharma, under his watchful eye.

The varna and ashrama in the dharma ideology refer only to men. For women—irrespective of caste—there was only *stri-dharma*, or obedience to man. The existence of the following narrative clearly indicates that the idea of female chastity was imposed on an otherwise free society.

☙ Shvetaketu's Law ❧
(Mahabharata)

Shvetaketu saw his mother in the arms of another man. When he complained to his father he was told, "All women are free to do as they wish." Horrified by this statement, Shvetaketu realized that it was thus impossible for any man to know who his biological father was. Shvetaketu was determined to set things right, so he decreed that henceforth a woman could have sexual relations only with her husband or with whomever he selected.

Kunti, the mother of the Pandavas, says in the Mahabharata, "In days of yore women went about freely doing as they pleased. There was no obligation to be faithful to their husbands." Anthropologists and feminists interpret this as a shift from matriarchal to patriarchal traditions. With this shift came stories to explain practices that the later patriarchy found unacceptable. For example, in the following story a conscious attempt is made to explain a woman's marriage to five men as an accident, not a conscious decision. It also endorses as noble a man's absolute obedience to his mother.

∽ The Marriage of Draupadi ∾
(Mahabharata)

Arjuna, the Pandava, won Draupadi's hand by winning an archery contest. He returned home and told his mother, "Guess what I won?" Without turning back, she replied, "Whatever it is, share it with your brothers." The obedient Arjuna therefore shared his wife with his four brothers.

The following story is another attempt to explain Draupadi's polyandry.

∽ Shiva Blesses Draupadi ∾
(Mahabharata)

Shiva was pleased with Draupadi's devotion and offered her anything she wanted. Draupadi wanted a husband with five qualities. "I want a husband who is noble, who is strong, who is a skilled warrior, who is handsome, and who is wise," she said. Shiva misunderstood her wish and said: "So be it. You will have five such husbands."

Although Lakshmi is the goddess of wealth she is considered fickle and whimsical. She needs to be domesticated and controlled if her grace is to be obtained (see Fig. 2.17). Hence she was always visualized at the feet of Vishnu, the keeper of cosmic order. In the cosmic household he is the divine husband and she is the divine wife. The idea of controlling the wife for the sake of domestic bliss is thus given divine resonance.

With the rise of patriarchy women were expected to do what their husbands told them. Those who obeyed were deified; those who did not were demonized. Narratives reflected a carrot-and-stick approach.

᎒ Vrinda's Chastity ᎒
(Shiva Purana)

Vrinda's chastity cast a shield of invulnerability around her husband, Jalandhara. This made him invincible in battle. Distressed, the gods sought the help of Vishnu, who seduced Vrinda by taking the form of her husband. By the time Vrinda realized that the man who posed as her husband was an imposter, it was too late. She had lost her chastity, and her husband lost the shield of invulnerability. He was killed by the gods and she became a widow.

Patriarchal Hinduism developed the concept of sati to ensure the fidelity of a wife. A sati is a woman who is so chaste that she comes to possess miraculous powers. Like the celibate man, the chaste woman became worthy of worship. She was equated to a goddess. The epic Ramayana drives the concept of female chastity to an extreme, where a slur against a woman's reputation becomes unforgivable.

᎒ Sita's Chastity ᎒
(Uttara Ramayana)

In keeping with her wifely duty Sita followed her husband to the forest and endured hardships for fourteen years. In the final year of her exile she was abducted by the rakshasa king Ravana. After a great battle Rama rescued her. But before accepting her back he demanded proof of her chastity. Sita jumped onto a pile of burning wood. The flames did not touch her, so pure was she. But despite his proof of chastity the people of Ayodhya were unwilling to accept a woman associated with another man as their queen. So Rama abandoned his wife, despite knowing that she was virtuous; he did not want his family name to be soiled in any way.

Even today during marriage ceremonies the bride is reminded of women who obeyed their husbands no matter what: Sita, who followed her husband to the forest; Mandodari, who remained faithful even though her husband, Ravana, was a rapist; Kunti, who, instructed by her husband, slept with gods to bear him children; Gandhari, who blindfolded herself to share her blind husband's handicap; Draupadi, who obeyed her husband, Arjuna, and married his brothers; Anasuya and Arundhati, who even the gods could not seduce. Strategic narratives that glorify female chastity have contributed in many ways to the internment of Hindu women within the household, bound by marriage and maternity.

In medieval India the idea of the sati, a chaste wife sharing the death of her husband, became immensely popular (see Fig. 2.18), a practice that aroused, and continues to arouse, outrage among Hindu social reformers. The practice had roots in the Brahmanical idea of absolute submission of female personality to that of her husband. It was probably a reaction to the Muslim invasion and a way of expressing "death over dishonor." Some scholars argue that the reason was economic—a way to prevent a childless widow from claiming her late husband's property. Widows who chose not to follow their dead husbands were not allowed to remarry and were forced to live a life of extreme austerity: They were prevented from wearing colored clothes, cosmetics, and ornaments and even had to shave their heads. While the living widow was considered inauspicious, the widow who leapt onto her husband's funeral pyre was deified. Her love and chastity, according to popular belief, prevented the flames from hurting her. In the Ramayana, Sita proves her chastity by going through a trial by fire. The Mahabharata refers to the wives of Krishna who became sati. Such fidelity was not demanded of husbands.

Strategic narratives play a very important role in social engineering. Stories such as the following established the relationship between father and son. The protagonist, Rama, expresses his divinity when he unquestioningly obeys his father.

༄ Three Boons for Kaikeyi ༄
(Ramayana)

Dashratha, king of Ayodhya, scion of the Raghu clan, had three wives. His second wife, Kaikeyi, was his favorite. She accompanied him even in battles. Once, in the thick of war, the axle of Dashratha's war chariot broke. Kaikeyi thrust her arm into the nave of the wheel and prevented the chariot from breaking apart. Pleased with her timely intervention, Dasharatha offered her two boons, which she decided to claim later.

In due course Dasharatha decided to crown Rama, his son by the senior queen, king. On the eve of the coronation, Kaikeyi demanded her two boons: that Rama go into exile and live in the forest as a hermit for fourteen years and that her son Bharata be crowned king in his place. Dasharatha had no choice but to keep his promise; Rama had no choice but to obey his father. While he left the city Rama said, "Men of the Raghu clan will die rather than break a promise or disobey their elders."

Strategic narratives explain not only artificial constructs but also natural phenomena.

ல How Mountains Came into Being ல
(Bhagavata Purana)

Once a demon called Hiranyaksha dragged the earth under the sea. Vishnu took the form of a boar, plunged into the sea, killed the demon, and rescued the earth. As Vishnu rose up from the bottom of the sea he embraced the earth passionately. The embrace caused the earth to fold, and thus mountains came into being.

The following story transforms the polestar into a symbol of steadfast devotion, as it explains its apparent stillness in the night sky.

ல Dhruva ல
(Folklore based on the Bhagavata Purana)

Dhruva wanted to sit on his father's lap but his stepmother would not allow it. "Your father may not let you sit on his lap, but God, who is father of the world, will," said his mother as she tried to console him. The boy took her words seriously. He ran away from home and went to the forest where he began meditating to invoke God. He refused to move until God gave him a place on his lap. Neither wind nor rain, hunger nor thirst, dented his determination. Finally Vishnu was pleased with Dhruva's stead-fast devotion and appeared before the boy and placed him on his lap. Dhruva transformed into the polestar. No one can move him from his celestial abode on the lap of Vishnu.

A story's function as a means of explanation lost value with the advent of science. However, even today etiological narratives help explain the otherwise inexplicable sacredness of a temple, a river, a lake, or a mountain. They tell us why a deity should be worshipped or why a ritual should be followed.

ᘓᔦ Donations for Venkateshwara ᔦᘓ
(Tirumalai Sthala Purana)

Lakshmi was once so angry with her consort, Vishnu, that she left his celestial abode, Vaikuntha, and came down to earth. To woo her back Vishnu came down too. But Lakshmi, who had taken up residence at Karavirapura, was too angry to return. Until she calmed down Vishnu decided to take up residence at Tirumalai, whose seven hills reminded him of the seven hoods of Adi Sesha, the serpent of time, on whose coils he rested at Vaikuntha.

To reside on the hills of Tirumalai Vishnu had to marry the local princess. To marry her he had to pay a heavy bridal price. Without Lakshmi, the goddess of wealth, by his side Vishnu had no money. So he took a loan from Kubera, the treasurer of the gods. Until he repays this loan Vishnu cannot leave his residence atop Tirumalai. As the lord of the hill he is revered as Venkateshwara.

To help Vishnu repay his debt devotees make offerings of money and gold at the temple. In gratitude Venkateshwara blesses them with worldly fortune. Thus the narrative helps establish a symbiotic relationship between the presiding deity and his devotees.

The following story attributes sacredness to a verse written by a poet; it transforms a human creation into a divine expression.

ᘓᔦ Jayadeva's Verse ᔦᘓ
(Folklore)

Jayadeva wrote the Gita Govinda, describing the amorous delights between the god Krishna and his beloved Radha. Jayadeva hesitated in writing a verse that showed the god as subservient to his beloved. While Jayadeva was away Krishna entered his house, took his form, and wrote the verse for him. Jayadeva realized Krishna wanted his devotees to see the true extent of his love for Radha. But the people of Puri refused to accept these verses. To see if Krishna really accepted these verses, the manuscript was kept in the sanctum sanctorum for a night along with the other verses used in the temple ceremonies. In the morning Jayadeva's manuscript was found atop all other manuscripts. Clearly it was the opinion of Krishna that the Gita Govinda best expressed his relationship with Radha.

In the eastern Indian state of Orissa is a temple that enshrines Krishna, his elder brother Balabhadra, and his younger sister Subhadra (see Fig. 2.19). The idols are made of wood, are quite crude, and seem incomplete by the standards of Indian art. The temple's tribal roots suggest these were probably ancient totems. But the popular explanation of the malformed images is that after Krishna's death a tree grew at the spot where he had been cremated. King Indradyumna, directed by a dream, found the trunk of this tree that was to be carved into the images of the three divine siblings. The wood was, however, too tough for any artisan to cut or carve. Then one day an old wood carver appeared before the king, saying he could carve the image if he was allowed to work in solitude. He warned the king that he would stop work if he was interrupted. The king agreed, and the wood carver locked himself in a room along with his tools and the tree trunk. Days passed. The artisan did not emerge from the room even for food. The sound of wood being cut and carved assured the king that work was progressing. Then one day the sound stopped. Indradyumna, too impatient to wait and terrified that the artisan was ill, barged into the workshop and angered the artisan, who was mixing paints. He disappeared and the images of Krishna, his brother Balabhadra, and his sister Subhadra remained incomplete.

THIS IN TERMS OF THAT

Viewing myths as allegories is a common way of rationalizing and domesticating myths. In an allegory the narrative is nothing but a medium for expressing something else—nothing more. The narrative has no value of its own; it is merely a vehicle for expressing something that is otherwise too abstract or profound or complex.

Most ancient cultures looked to the stars to solve the mysteries of earthly life. These peoples believed that stars charted the course of human existence or expressed the will of the gods. The wisdom the people acquired by observing the movements of the stars was transmitted through mythic narratives.

Ancient Vedic astronomers noted that the rising sun moved northward along the horizon for six months (causing the days to grow longer and warmer), and then moved southward for the remaining six (causing the days to grow shorter and colder). It was as if two opposing forces were churning the cosmos. The ancients called the two forces devas and asuras (lords of light and darkness, often mistranslated as gods and demons). The northern movement of the rising sun was called *Uttarayana* and was associated with the devas; the southern movement was called *Dakshinayana* and was associated with the asuras. During Uttarayana the sun moved into the house of Capricorn, which became the symbol of fertility and growth (as Capricorn was a combination of an elephant, goat, and fish). During Dakshinayana the sun moved into the house of Cancer, which became the symbol of infertility and bondage (crabs don't let other crabs leave the basket).

Like Uttarayana, Hindus consider the waxing half of the lunar month to be auspicious. The following narrative explains why, and also attempts to establish a relationship between the moon and the twenty-seven lunar mansions or asterisms, known in Hindu astrology as *nakshatras*.

౽ Chandra and the Nakshatras ౿
(Somnath Sthala Purana)

The moon god Chandra was married to twenty-seven daughters of the priest king Daksha, but he preferred only one: Rohini. Daksha warned Chandra to treat all his daughters equally. When Chandra ignored this warning Daksha cursed him to lose his potency and wither away. Distraught, Chandra invoked Shiva, who restored his potency.

It is said that Chandra agreed to visit each of his wives at least once a month; he waxes every time he approaches Rohini and wanes every time he moves away from her. The nakshatra Rohini is also viewed as a celestial doe chased by the constellation Orion (known to Hindu astronomers as Mrigashiras or the celestial buck). The belt of Orion is considered to be the arrow shot at Mrigashiras either by the deer hunter, by Mrigavadhya (the Dog Star Sirius), or the bowman Dhanu (the zodiac Sagittarius). This relationship is expressed in the following narrative.

౽ Rudra and Prajapati ౿
(Shatapatha Brahmana)

Prajapati experienced lust for the first woman he created. The woman, called Ushas, ran, taking the form of a doe. Prajapati pursued her as a buck. The assembled divinities were horrified at this display of unbridled lust by a father for his daughter. They called for Rudra, for only he dared punish the father. Rudra, the hunter, raised his bow and shot Prajapati, injuring him and causing him to abandon the chase.

The next story explains the relationship between the seven stars of the Great Bear constellation (known to Hindus as Sapta Rishi), the star Alkor (known as Arundhati) which is close to the Great Bear constellation, and the Pleiades (known as Krittikas), which stands independent of the Great Bear in the opposite direction and is associated in astrology with violence, ruin, and disgrace.

✑ Sapta Rishis and Their Wives ✑
(Mahabharata)

The seven cosmic seers, the mind-born sons of Brahma known as the Sapta Rishis, were guardians of the Veda. Their seven wives were faithful and obedient spouses. The fire god Agni desired all seven of them but was kept at bay by the power of their chastity.

On a particularly cold winter's day the seven women bathed in the river. The water was freezing so they decided to warm themselves before the fire. Arundhati, wife of the seer Vasistha, warned the women not to go to the fire without putting on the emblems of marriage. But the women ignored her warning and went to the fire altar. The fire god took advantage of this lapse and made love to them with heat and light. Soon the seers discovered that their wives, all except Arundhati, were pregnant. While accusing the women of infidelity, the men drove their wives out of the house. The wives became ferocious autonomous women known as Krittikas who wandered in the wilderness, homeless and aimless. Only Arundhati remained in the hermitage of the seven seers.

The Krittikas shed the unwanted embryo that was nurtured, fused, and transformed by the fire god into the celestial warlord Skanda, who was also known as Kartikeya, son of the Krittikas. The Krittikas wanted to harm Skanda, as he was the cause of their misery, but they were overcome with maternal affection when they saw him. Skanda decreed that the Krittikas had the right to harm unborn and newborn children unless women appeased them with prayers and referred to them as mothers, or Matrikas.

Often it is difficult to distinguish between the Arundhati star and the star in the Great Bear constellations that the Hindu astronomers called Vasistha. This observation made the star a symbol of Arundhati's unshakable chastity.

Like astronomical phenomena, metaphysical ideas are difficult to communicate directly. One needs stories and symbols to do so. Subscribers to this thought believe that over time simpleminded people let the stories and symbols overpower the underlying idea and become more important than what they represented.

An image of Lakshmi, the goddess of wealth, is found in most Hindu households and business establishments (see Fig. 2.20). By placing this rather intense symbol of fortune and fertility the devotee visually establishes a direct communication of his or her desire with the cosmos. Allegory makes the image and attributes of Lakshmi comprehensible. The red sari of the goddess and her location in a lotus pond link her to fertility. Her upward-pointing palm indicates grace, while the palm pointing downward indicates generosity. The pot from which gold flows indicates transmission of wealth that gives value to currency. The elephants symbolize power. The image befits the goddess who bestows wealth and fortune.

The ultimate aim of Hinduism is to realize one's true nature, which is in essence divine. The soul of the jiva, the *jiva-atma,* is like a drop of seawater that needs to realize it is part of the ocean; the ocean is *param-atma,* God itself. The relationship between jiva-atma and param-atma is explained allegorically as that of a beloved and a lover. When apart there is unhappiness; when in union there is joy. The following narrative is often interpreted as the milkmaids symbolizing jiva-atma and Krishna symbolizing param-atma.

༄ Krishna's Rasa Leela ༄
(Gita Govinda)

On full-moon nights in the meadows on the banks of the river Yamuna, Krishna would play his flute, beckoning the milkmaids of his village. They would come, secretly, risking their reputations, and make a circle around him and dance to his tune, losing themselves completely in the performance. When this happened it seemed to each milkmaid that Krishna danced with her alone. Sometimes the milkmaids boasted that Krishna belonged to them. When this happened Krishna would disappear, making the women experience the pain of separation. Krishna would only return when this need to possess him was abandoned.

The following narrative shows how unconditional surrender to God liberates the jiva from the mire of samsara. Here the bull elephant represents the jiva entrapped by the sorrows (the crocodile) of the samsara (the lake) because he succumbed to the temptations of the material world (water sports with the cow elephants). He is rescued when he stops struggling and offers a lotus flower to Vishnu, the supreme godhead.

ᖆᓇ The Rescue of the Elephant King ᖆᓇ
(Bhagavata Purana)

Gajendra, the elephant king, entered a lotus pond to play and make love to his harem of cow elephants. Unfortunately, he was attacked by the crocodile king who lived in that lake. The crocodile caught Gajendra's hind leg and began dragging him under water. The elephant king tried hard to break free but failed. Finally he just let go. He picked a lotus with his trunk, held it high, and offered it to Vishnu, appealing for help. Instantly Vishnu appeared riding his eagle. He liberated Gajendra by striking the crocodile king with his discus.

The allegorical approach to a narrative helped many come to terms with apparently obscene stories of gods and goddesses.

∽ Shiva's Erect Manhood ∽
(Shiva Purana)

Shiva wandered into a forest naked, blissfully unaware of his erect manhood. The wives of the sages who lived in this forest ran after him in lust. Their husbands blamed Shiva for the wantonness of their wives. Enraged, they castrated Shiva. Shiva's manhood turned into a pillar of fire that threatened to destroy the world. Upon realizing their mistake the sages prayed to the Goddess, who contained the fire by capturing the raging phallus in her womb.

Shiva's erect manhood is not the result of sexual arousal. It is causeless; an expression of pure, unadulterated bliss, or ananda. This state of ecstasy is inherent when the consciousness is unfettered by the ego and the mind, is free of all adulterations, and realizes the absolute truth about material and spiritual reality. The unenlightened sages view divinity through the limited perspective of their ego-dominated consciousness. Castration is catastrophic as it breaks the link between spiritual and material reality, a link that is vital if world is to exist. The world exists only when it is perceived. Perception occurs only if there is awareness. Awareness occurs only if there is consciousness. Consciousness is intangible. Consciousness is spiritual reality.

According to the Padma Purana milkmaids were once bathing in a pond when Krishna stole their clothes (see Fig.2.21). He returned them only when the women stepped out of the pond and displayed their nakedness to him in love and without shame. This story is often explained allegorically. Clothing is interpreted as the mental modifications stemming from the ego that takes one away from the divine (Krishna). The lake represents the material world. Liberation from the material world, which is union with the divine, is attained only when these clothes are abandoned.

METAPHORS OF THE MIND

There are things in this world that we would rather not talk about, but they demand expression. In such cases myth becomes a safety valve of culture, expressing unacceptable ideas in an acceptable manner. Stories allow the imagination to flirt with what is forbidden in reality. Take the following story, for example, which is from the Mahabharata.

◡◠ Kunti's Magic Formula ◠◡
(Mahabharata)

The princess Kunti served the sage Durvasa well when he visited her father's house. Durvasa was pleased and gave her a magic formula with which she could call upon any deva and have a child by him. To test the formula Kunti called upon Surya, the sun god, and had a son by him. As she was unmarried and did not want to soil her reputation, she put the child in a basket and left it to the river's whim.

Kunti married Pandu, king of Hastinapur. Unfortunately, he was afflicted with a curse that prevented him from making love to his wife. So Kunti called upon Dharma, the god of righteousness, Vayu, the god of wind, and Indra, the rain god and king of the devas, and bore three sons who were addressed by all as Pandavas, the sons of Pandu.

The story may be seen as a metaphorical retelling of premarital and extramarital childbearing—the former as a result of youthful indiscretion with a houseguest, the latter to resolve the issue of succession because of a husband's impotence. By making Kunti's lovers devas the narrator projects an unacceptable reality onto the realm of the gods. The audience comprehends the subtext and the social taboos against premarital and extramarital sex.

Transformation of a repressed desire into myth is not necessarily a conscious process. Freud saw myth and ritual as an unconscious expression of repressed dreams of a community that explained universal taboos against incest and patricide. In the Greek myth of Oedipus, who unknowingly killed his father and married his mother and who blinded himself to atone for his unintentional crimes, Freud saw the universal unspoken need of the son to compete with and triumph over the father for maternal affection. To him this Oedipus complex formed the foundation of (Judaic) monotheism—a guilty response to the killing of the founding patriarch (Moses) and enjoying what was rightfully his (the promised land). To Freud religion was nothing but neurosis, and the answer to myth lay in the unconscious.

While Greek mythology is full of stories in which a son is responsible for the death of his father or a father figure (Chronos castrates Uranus; Zeus kills Chronus; Perseus kills his grandfather, Acrisius; Aegeus killed himself, believing his son Theseus to be dead; Jason's wife, Medea, kills his stepfather Pelias), such narratives are not found in Hindu scriptures. This indicates that the Oedipus complex suggested in myth is a cultural, not a universal, phenomenon.

Tales in Hindu scriptures suggest a reverse-Oedipal, or Yayati, complex. In this case the father destroys the son in order to have his way.

༄ The Sons of Yayati ༄
(Mahabharata)

When Devayani learned that her husband, Yayati, had secretly married her maid, Sarmishtha, and that the maid had borne him two sons, Devayani ran to her father the asura-priest, Shukra, who cursed Yayati to become old and impotent. When he realized the implications of the curse, Shukra modified it, stating that Yayati would regain his youth and potency if one of his sons willingly bore the burden of the curse. The youngest son, Puru, agreed to become old and impotent so that his father could enjoy life. Puru regained his youth and earned the gratitude of his father years later when, after indulging his senses in every way, Yayati realized the ephemeral nature of material things and decided it was time to let go and grow old.

A descendent of Puru, Devavrata also has to waylay his aspirations for the pleasure of his father.

ᴄᴏ Devavrata's Vow of Celibacy ᴄᴏ
(Mahabharata)

Shantanu wanted to marry the fisherwoman Satyavati, but she refused to accept the proposal until he promised that her sons, not Devavrata, Shantanu's son by his first wife, Ganga, would inherit his throne. To make his father happy Devavrata gave up his claim to the throne. But this did not satisfy Satyavati. "I want a guarantee that your descendents will not fight the descendents of my sons for the throne," she told Devavrata. He gave her the guarantee the only way possible: He took a vow of celibacy. This vow earned him the wrath of his ancestors, for he would not facilitate their rebirth. It also doomed him to an eternity in the land of the dead, as without descendents there would be no one in the world to facilitate his own rebirth. By condemning himself to such misery for the sake of his father's happiness, Devavrata earned the admiration of the gods, who renamed him Bhisma, "he who took a terrible vow."

In the Greek narratives sons triumph over fathers, humans triumph over gods, the individual triumphs over society. The one who goes against authority and tradition is celebrated. The rebel, whether it is Prometheus (who opposes Zeus), Heracles (who stands up to Hera), or Ulysses (who challenges Poseidon), is deified. In Hindu narratives the hero is one who submits to the will of the father, society, and tradition. Obedience is the highest virtue. Rama is *maryada purushottama,* the perfect upholder of social values, because he always does what is expected of him. That is why he is God.

Not everyone appreciates Freud's rereading of myths in terms of sexual anxiety. Some people do not agree with the view that all ritual and religion emerges from the desire to recall, remember, and repeat primal crimes that apparently marked the dawn of civilization in order to come to terms with them. Indeed Freud's mythography has been deemed reductive and phallocentric, focusing on penis envy with an almost misogynist zeal.

Freud's most famous disciple, Jung, was less concerned with the origin of anxiety and more concerned with the resolution of anxiety. For Jung the task of life is to come to terms with the contents of the individual unconscious (expressed in dreams and visions) by relating them to those of the collective unconscious (expressed in myth). According to Jung the unconscious is made up of:

- Ego (the conscious aspect of the psyche that bestows identity on and purpose to an individual)
- Shadow (the unconscious aspect of the psyche that the ego tends to reject or ignore)
- Anima/animus (the unconscious intuitive/rational female/male that complements the ego)
- Self (the ultimate potential of being)

Jung saw these parts of the unconscious manifesting as characters in every myth. He called these characters *archetypal images*—reflections of the archetype, or permanent patterns of understanding located in the collective unconscious. Jung believed that through narratives, symbols, and rituals the ego, with the aid of anima/animus, could confront the shadow and realize the self, a process he called *individuation*. One who undergoes the process of individuation is a hero and is visualized by the rest as an ideal, or a god. Mythologists like Joseph Campbell took this idea further and identified the self with the soul and the collective unconsciousness with divinity, transforming individuation into mysticism. Narrative details did not matter to Jung; they only helped in identifying the archetypal image.

Based on Jung's methods, the following story can be seen as the coming of age of a man and his emergence from the shadow of women. In this journey the hero, Arjuna, moves from a woman who shares her affections with his brothers and who discards him for interrupting her sojourn with another man (Draupadi), to a woman who rapes him (Uloopi), to a woman who loves him but is unwilling to share his life (Chitrangada), and finally to a woman who loves him so much that she is willing to be abducted by him (Subhadra). In folk versions of this narrative from Tamil Nadu, Arjuna is accompanied by his guide Krishna, who, as Arjuna's wise teacher and friend, even makes him rape a rebellious warrior woman called Ali by taking the form of a serpent and slipping into her bed while she is asleep.

ᴄᴏ Arjuna's Exile ᴄᴏ
(Mahabharata)

To avoid quarrels between them, the Pandava brothers had agreed that each one of them would cohabit with their common wife, Draupadi, for a year and stay away for four years. Anyone who broke this agreement would spend a year in self-imposed exile. Arjuna broke the rule when he entered Draupadi's chambers in search of his bow while she was with his eldest brother.

During his exile Arjuna went on a pilgrimage. While bathing in a river the serpent maiden Uloopi abducted him and forced him to give her a child. Then he met the princess Chitrangada in the kingdom of Manipur. They fell in love, but her father only let them marry on the condition that all children born of this union would belong to him. Arjuna then visited the city of his friend and cousin Krishna, where he fell in love with Krishna's sister Subhadra. Since the elders of the city were not in favor of their marriage he abducted her and took her to his city.

When Draupadi had agreed to be the common wife of the Pandavas she had demanded that no other woman should live in their house. With great difficulty, some cajoling, and some trickery Krishna and Arjuna managed to convince Draupadi to share her house with her cowife Subhadra.

Jung believed that symbols captured ideas too profound to be expressed in words. They are conscious expressions of subconscious feelings. The meanings are not obvious or direct; they are hidden deep within and are open to great speculation. One has to meditate on the idea until it sparks a profound insight into the deeper meaning of the cosmos and a better understanding of the self.

A common representation of the Goddess is the Shri Chakra, which is a set of upward- and downward-pointing triangles intersecting each other in a lotuslike circle (see Fig. 2.22). Rather than being dismissed as a meaningless fertility talisman, Jungian mythography demands meditating on the image and trying to fathom its meaning. The downward-pointing triangle represents the female generative organ, the womb. The upward-pointing triangle represents the male generative organ, the phallus. The intersection represents creation, the flowering of the cosmos like a lotus emerging from the sea of entropy. The circle represents samsara. The multiple triangles heighten the interaction between God and Goddess, spirit and material, and intensify the divine aura within the Hindu paradigm. What emerges is Shri: authority, affluence, abundance, and auspiciousness desired by all living things.

Like Freud and Jung, Claude Lévi-Strauss believed that the answer to myth lay in the unconscious. Unlike Freud he did not see myth as a tool to revisit and reconcile with primordial shameful acts (incest and patricide). Unlike Jung he did not focus only on the symbols that emerge out of narratives, nor did he allow for individual interpretations. For Lévi-Strauss every myth had a structure that established the relationship between the various units of myth (Jung called these archetypal images; Lévi-Strauss called them *mythemes*), just as grammar establishes the relationship between words in any language. A study of these structures in a whole set of myths reveals a common denominator: the need of a community to impose order on the disorder of the environment and to reconcile conflicts, such as those between nature and culture. This school of mythography is called *structuralism*. In it the details of the myth matter less than the underlying structure. It strives to be the invariant, the common denominator, among superficial differences. This invariant is how the mind perceives and copes with reality. As the audience becomes familiar with the narrative the structure subtly resolves in the unconscious the conflicts perceived by the conscious. Myths are thus devices to think with and ways of classifying and organizing reality. This, rather than the recounting of any particular tale, is the point of the myth—hence Lévi-Strauss' remark that "myths get thought in man unbeknownst to him."

The following table shows how the many plots in the Ramayana try to reconcile the struggle between nature and culture. Rama represents culture, an upholding of dharma that restrains the instincts of sex and violence, while Ravana represents nature, submitting to the law of the jungle and the instincts of sex and violence (see Table 29).

An overview of Hindu narratives shows very clearly that there is an obsession with explaining an event as a reaction to a past event, one that occurred in this life or in the one before. This structure drives home the idea of karma, the belief that all beings are obliged to experience the reactions of their actions, either in this life or the next. This belief forms the foundation of the Hindu worldview (see Table 30).

TABLE 29. COMPARISON OF RAMA AND RAVANA IN THE RAMAYANA

Rama	Ravana
Father and mother are Kshatriyas (members of the warrior caste)	Father is a brahmana (priest-philosopher), while mother is a rakshasa (barbarian) princess
Gives up his kingdom (Ayodhya) in favor of his half-brother (Bharata)	Kills his half-brother (Kubera) and usurps his kingdom (Lanka)
Has only one wife	Has many wives
Obeys his father by agreeing to go into exile for 14 years	Disobeys his father and mother and fights his brother
Renounces his wife in deference to the will of his people, as they do not want a woman of soiled reputation as their queen	Abducts Sita, the wife of another man, despite popular dissent
Restores the chastity of women such as Ahalya, who is turned into stone by her husband because of her adultery	Molests women such as Rambha and Vedavati
Supports the yagna of the rishis	Disrupts the yagna of the rishis
Upholds caste values by following the path of his father as warrior and king	Breaks caste values by moving away from his father's path, abandoning the way of the brahmana, and becoming a warrior and king
Upholds social law even at the cost of personal happiness	Follows the law of the jungle that might is right

The concept of the Goddess in Hinduism can be understood not through one image or one narrative but by looking at all images and all narratives and the relationship between each. No singular form of the Goddess can encapsulate the profound secrets of samsara that she embodies. Collectively the forms project the object

TABLE 30. ACTIONS AND THEIR REACTIONS IN THE MAHABHARATA

Action	Reaction
Ambalika becomes pale when Vyasa makes love to her	Ambalika's child, Pandu, father of the Pandavas, is born an albino
Ambika shuts her eyes when Vyasa makes love to her	Ambika's child, Dhritarashtra, uncle of Ambalika, becomes pale when Vyasa makes love to her
A princess constantly craves the embrace of her sage husband	She is reborn as Draupadi, who is given five husbands
Arjuna is proud of his archery, Bhima of his gluttony, Nakula of his beauty, Sahadeva of his wisdom	All four Pandavas are denied entry into Indra's paradise
Arjuna refuses to make love to Urvashi on the grounds that she was married to his ancestor, Pururava	Arjuna loses his manhood for a year
Gandhari accidentally crushes one hundred turtle eggs when she is a child	Gandhari, wife of Dhritarashtra, witnesses the death of her one hundred sons, the Kauravas, at the hands of the Pandavas
Pandu accidentally kills a sage and his wife while they are making love	Pandu is cursed that death will strike if he ever makes love to his wives, Kunti and Madri
Sudyumna trespasses in the woods where the goddess Parvati is sporting with her lord Shiva	Sudyumna becomes a woman called Ila and bears a son called Pururava, ancestor of the Pandavas

that is experienced in life with which the subject who experiences life must come to terms in his or her quest for self-actualization, self-gratification, and ultimately self-realization.

Chinnamastika and Lalita-Tripurasundari represent nature in its raw and pleasant forms (see Fig. 1.9 and Fig. 1.10). Kali and Alakshmi represent the untamed, inauspicious, and undesired parts of nature, while Gauri and Lakshmi (see Fig. 2.20) represent the parts that are tamed, auspicious, and desired. Durga (see Fig. 1.23) stands where the circle of nature and the square of culture meet, unleashing her violent traits in a disciplined way against the enemy, not randomly like Kali. Saraswati (see Fig. 1.27), the serene wisdom of nature, marks the center of the circle and the square (see the diagram below).

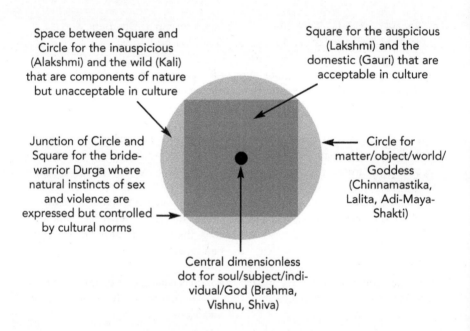

Space between Square and Circle for the inauspicious (Alakshmi) and the wild (Kali) that are components of nature but unacceptable in culture

Square for the auspicious (Lakshmi) and the domestic (Gauri) that are acceptable in culture

Junction of Circle and Square for the bride-warrior Durga where natural instincts of sex and violence are expressed but controlled by cultural norms

Circle for matter/object/world/Goddess (Chinnamastika, Lalita, Adi-Maya-Shakti)

Central dimensionless dot for soul/subject/individual/God (Brahma, Vishnu, Shiva)

Linking Sacred Idea, Imagery and Geometry

In households the goddesses Lakshmi and Gauri are worshipped. Alakshmi is beseeched to stay out. Followers of Tantra who seek the truth beyond social constructs worship Kali and Chinnamastika, as the former is reality outside the boundaries of social construct while the latter is reality when social construct collapses. The following table compares and contrasts the three manifestations of Shakti. This brings to light how the three manifestations embody different aspects of nature (see Table 31).

TABLE 31. COMPARISON OF KALI, GAURI, AND DURGA

Kali	Gauri	Durga
Associated with death	Associated with childbirth	Associated with defense
Cackles and dances wildly in crematoriums and battlefields	Speaks softly, listens to all woes, and under-stands all problems	Is soft and gentle yet firm and distant
Crone	Mother	Virgin
Destructive	Creative and maternal	Protective
Has no home	Is the mistress of a joyful household	Seen in battlefields
Her body is shriveled	Her body is soft and maternal	Her body is sensuous
Her eyes are ferocious and she sticks out her blood-soaked tongue	Her eyes are loving and she smiles with maternal affection	Her eyes are forbidding
Her hair is unbound and unadorned	Her hair is anointed with oil, arranged in a top-knot, and adorned with flowers	Her hair is unbound but bedecked with bridal jewelry
Her mannerisms are wild	Her manner is is demure and domestic	Her manner is that of a disciplined warrior
Holds skulls, bones, decapitated bodies, and severed limbs	Holds babies, plants, flowers, and conch shells	Holds weapons
Is associated with jackals, hounds, and scorpions	Is associated with the cow and the cat	Is associated with lions and tigers

TABLE 31. COMPARISON OF KALI, GAURI, AND DURGA (CONTINUED)

Kali	Gauri	Durga
Offered sour and pungent food like lime and chilies	Offered sweet food like jaggery and milk	Offered the blood of male animals like buffaloes, billy goats, roosters, and rams
Represents the wilderness, where all urges are untamed	Represents culture, where all urges are restrained	Represents the junction of culture and nature, where sexual and violent urges are channeled with discretion for the good of culture
The dark one	The radiant one	The inaccessible one
Tramples her consort	Sits on the lap of her consort	Never directly associated with a consort
Wears no clothes (raw, untamed fertility)	Drapes herself in a green sari (realized and domesticated fertility) and adorns herself with the sixteen love charms of the married woman	Wears a red sari (potential fertility), bridal jewelry, and armor

The Freudian, Jungian, and structuralist schools are extremely useful in interpreting myth, as long as they are used loosely, serving as guidelines rather than dogmas. No single method offers a solution to all narratives.

CONCLUSION

Myths may be mere histories, social charters, allegories, metaphors, expressions of the unconscious, and much more, gathering layers of meaning as they are passed from generation to generation. Consider, for example, the Hindu epic the

Ramayana, which was written in Sanskrit between 200 B.C.E. and A.D. 200 and retold in over three hundred languages, inspiring poetry, drama, mime, and ritual in India and beyond. The Ramayana can be viewed as a historical record, as an allegory, or as a political document. It has been successfully interpreted using psychoanalytical methods and the tools of structuralism (See Table 32).

No single method of interpretation is complete. It is through the richness of interpretation that a narrative, symbol, or ritual acquires its mythic power.

TABLE 32. DIFFERENT INTERPRETATIONS OF THE RAMAYANA

School	Interpretation
Allegorical	Devotion (Hanuman) can unite the individual soul (Sita) with the cosmic soul (Rama), which are separated by the ego (Ravana)
Euhemerist	A bard's record of the life of an ancient Hindu king called Rama, who introduced Vedic culture to South India and who was later deified as an incarnation of Vishnu
Freudian	A projection of the desire to kill the father (Dasaratha) onto a father figure (Ravana) who deprives man (Rama) of what he rightfully deserves (Ayodhya/Sita)
Jungian	Self-actualizing journey of a hero: Rama is the ego, Ravana his shadow, Sita the positive anima, Surpanakha the negative anima, Hanuman the animus
Political	An epic that imposes the Brahmanical ideology of varna-ashrama-dharma, which compels all people to live their lives following duties determined by their station in society and stage in life
Structuralist	An epic that resolves the conflict of nature (the jungle law followed by Ravana) and culture (the code of civilization upheld by Rama)

Glossary

Agni: Fire god.

apsara: Nymph who seduces sages.

artha: Worldly wealth.

Arya: Nobleman who respects dharma, practices yoga, performs yagna, and respects the Vedas.

ashrama: Stage of life: student, householder, retired teacher, and hermit.

asura: Enemies of the devas; demons who live in the nether regions; sons of Kashyapa born of Diti and Danu.

ayonija: Born without being nurtured in the womb.

Ayurveda: Ancient Indian medical system.

Ayyappa: Celibate son of Shiva and Vishnu who is worshipped in the southern Indian state of Kerala. *See* Manikantha and Hari-Hara-suta.

Bhagavan: God; he who rotates the cycle of life.

Brahma: Creator; sits on a lotus, chants the Vedas from his four heads, and holds implements to perform yagna in his four hands; not worshipped because he desired his daughter, the primal female.

brahmacharya: Chaste student life; first stage of life.

Brahman: The impersonal divine principle.

Brahmana: Ritual texts based on Vedic hymns.

brahmana: Highest ritual caste; priest and philosopher; one who teaches society.

Brihaspati: Lord of the planet Jupiter; guru of the devas.

Budha: Lord of the planet Mercury; son of the moon god.

chakra: Gateway to occult knowledge.

chandala: Lowest rank in the Hindu caste hierarchy; one who takes care of crematoriums.

Chandra: Moon god.

Daksha: A mind-born son of Brahma; father-in-law of all the gods, including Shiva; lord of Dakshinachara.

Dakshinachara: Conventional, mainstream, ritualistic way of life based on rituals and philosophies inspired by the Vedas; this approach views the material world as a wild and illusory one that needs to be restrained through dharma and yoga.

demiurge: Primal source.

deva: Enemy of the asuras; gods who live in the celestial regions; sons of Kashyapa, born of Aditi.

dharma: Social order based on the doctrine of duty instituted and maintained by Vishnu.

Draupadi: Common wife of the five Pandavas.

Drona: Preceptor of the Kuru clan; teacher of the Kauravas and Pandavas; friend and later foe of Drupada.

Durga: Warrior manifestation of the mother goddess; she is dressed in red, rides a lion, and bears weapons in her eight arms to kill the buffalo demon.

gandharva: Celestial musicians; companions of the apsaras.

Ganesha: Elephant-headed son of Gauri; remover of obstacles; adored as a bachelor in South India but has two wives in North Indian traditions.

Gauri: Wife of Shiva; another name for Parvati; radiant and maternal manifestation of the mother goddess.

grihastha: Householder; second stage of life.

Hanuman: Monkey god who serves Rama.

Hari-Hara-suta: Another name for the celibate son of Shiva and Vishnu. *See* Ayyappa and Manikantha.

Hindu: Generic term for a set of beliefs, customs, and practices that evolved in the Indian subcontinent and later spread to Southeast Asia; has two approaches to life, the Vedic and tantric; is divided into three theistic schools based on the worship of Shiva (Shaiva), Vishnu (Vaishnava), and the mother goddess (Shakta).

Indra: King of the devas; god of the sky, rain, and thunder.

itihasa: Legendary history; Ramayana, Mahabharata, and its appendix Harivamsa.

Jainism: The atheistic religion based on austerities and nonviolence that rejects Vedic ritualism and helps the aspirant generate good karma, enabling him or her to attain kaivalya (freedom from the cycle of life).

jati: Caste.

kaivalya: Omniscience that liberates one from the cycle of life; Jain concept of liberation from the cycle of life; isolation from impurities.

Kali: Wild and fierce manifestation of the mother goddess.

kama: Desire, sensual pleasures.

Kandarpa: God of love and lust who wields a sugarcane bow, shoots flowery darts, and rides a parrot.

karma: Action one performs and the reactions to those actions that one is bound to experience either in this life or in the next.

Kartikeya: Son of Shiva; the warlord who killed an asura on the seventh day of his life; rides a peacock, wields a lance, and has a rooster insignia on his banner; is said to be a bachelor in North India but has two wives (Valli and Sena) in South India.

Kaurava: Villain in the Mahabharata; enemy of the Pandavas who believes he has a greater right to the throne of Hastinapur because his father, Dhritarashtra, though blind and deemed unfit to rule, was the elder son of Vichitravirya.

kimnara: Literally, "what men"; quasi-men; queer beings.

kimpurusha: Literally, "what men"; quasi-men; queer beings.

Krishna: Human incarnation of Vishnu who established dharma in the third quarter of the world cycle; renowned for his beauty, charm, and his winsome wiliness; godhead personified.

Krittika: Nursemaids of Kartikeya.

kshatriya: Second highest ritual caste; warrior and administrator; one who rules and protects society.

Kuru: The clan of warriors to which the Pandavas and Kauravas belong.

Lakshmana: Rama's younger brother.

Lakshmi: Goddess of wealth and fortune; wears a red sari, wears gold ornaments, sits on a lotus, holds lotuses and a pot in her hand.

linga: Phallus.

Mahabharata: Epic based on the struggle between the Pandavas and Kauravas for the throne of Hastinapur.

manava: Children of Manu; humans.

Mangal: Lord of the planet Mars; Kartikeya.

Manikantha: Another name for the celibate son of Shiva and Vishnu. *See* Ayyappa and Hari-Hara-suta.

mantra: Sacred or mystical chant.

Manu: Father of humankind.

Maya: The idea of maya embodied in a female form; another name for the Goddess.

maya: Delusion; misinterpretation of sensory stimuli by an unenlightened mind.

Mohini: Celestial enchantress.

moksha: Hindu concept of liberation from the cycle of life.

Murugan: Another name for Kartikeya that is popular in Tamil Nadu.

naga: Serpent being who lives in subterranean realms.

Naraka: Subterranean realm of the asuras.

Narasimha: Half-man, half-lion incarnation of Vishnu.

nirvana: Buddhist concept of liberation from the cycle of life; blowing out of impermanent constructs.

paap: Conduct that goes against dharma and generates unfavorable karma.

Pandavas: Heroes in the Mahabharata; enemies of the Kauravas who believe they have a greater right to the throne of Hastinapur because their father, Pandu, though the younger son of Vichitravirya, was crowned king.

parampara: Tradition.

Parvati: Consort of Shiva; princess of the mountains; succeeded in making the hermit Shiva a householder.

pitr: Forefather.

Prajapati: Father of beings; another name for Brahma or his manifestation Kashyapa.

prakriti: Nature; another term for material reality, or samsara.

Prithu: The sovereign who domesticated the earth and established dharma; incarnation of Vishnu.

punya: Conduct that upholds dharma and generates favorable karma.

Purana: Ancient chronicles of gods, kings, and sages written between 500 and 1500.

Puru: Ancestor of the Kurus; accepted his father Yayati's old age so that Yayati could enjoy the pleasures of youth.

Purusha: Primal man; another term for spiritual reality.

purushartha: Validation of human life through ethical (dharma), economic (artha), sensual (kama), and spiritual (moksha) activities.

Radha: Beloved of Krishna; a milkmaid; believed to be the wife of another man in one tradition and the Shakti of Krishna in another.

rakshasa: Demon; barbarian; wild forest spirit.

Ramayana: Epic based on the life of Rama.

Ravana: King of the rakshasas; villain of the Ramayana; abducted Sita and was killed by Rama.

rishi: Seer; wise man who transmitted cosmic knowledge to humankind through Vedic hymns.

samadhi: Yogic term for breaking free from the cycle of life by discriminating between material and spiritual reality.

samsara: Material reality; wheel of existence; cycle of rebirths; nature; mundane world of time and space, name, and form.

sanyasa: Hermit; fourth and final stage of life.

Saraswati: Goddess of learning and the arts; consort of Brahma; she is draped in a white sari and holds a lute, a pen, and a book and rides a gander.

Sati: First wife of Shiva who killed herself when her father, Daksha, insulted her husband by not inviting him to the sacrifice.

sati: Chaste wife who kills herself on her husband's funeral pyre.

shakti: Energy, matter, strength, power.

Shakti: Goddess who embodies material energy; personification of divine power.

Shiva: Cosmic hermit; god of destruction; wears animal skins, smears his body with ash, meditates on icy mountains, dances in crematoriums, smokes hemp, carries a trident, and rides a bull; world-renouncing aspect of godhead.

shruti: Divine revelations; the Vedas.

shudra: Lowest ritual caste; servant and laborer; one who serves society.

Shukra: Lord of the planet Venus; guru of the asuras.

siddhi: Mystical powers that enable a person to manipulate cosmic forces.

Sita: Chaste wife of Rama.

smriti: Scriptures based on human memory that inform humans how to live wholesome lives; includes the Puranas and the Shastras.

Sthala Purana: Local chronicle.

Subramanium: Another name for Kartikeya that is popular in South India.

Sugriva: King of the monkeys, or vanars.

Surya: Sun god.

swarga: Celestial realms; abode of the devas.

Tantra: Occult side of Hinduism (*see* Vamachara) that views the flesh and the material world as the medium through which the truth can be realized.

Upanishad: Philosophical treatise based on the Vedas that seeks the ultimate truth.

vaishya: Third highest ritual caste; farmer, herdsman, craftsman, or trader; one who provides for society.

vama: Left; also refers to women.

Vamachara: Unconventional, occult, tantric way of life.

vanaprastha: Retired teacher; third stage of life.

vanara: Monkey; literally means "forest dweller."

varna: Four ritual castes: those who teach, protect, provide, and serve society.

Varuna: Vedic god of morality who later became renowned as the lord of the sea.

Vedas: Collection of hymns that capture the absolute truth.

Vedic: Ritualistic, speculative, and mainstream Hinduism, in which nature is viewed as something wild to be regulated by dharma and the material world is seen as a delusion that overwhelms the senses. Truth can be realized only through mental control (yoga). *See* Dakshinachara.

Vena: King who abandoned dharma.

vira: Heroic being; brave conqueror of spiritual or material realms; refers to both the sage and the warrior.

Vishnu: Cosmic king; god who sustains the world by instituting and maintaining dharma; he adorns himself with silk, garlands, jewels, and sandal paste and rests on a serpent and rides an eagle; world-affirming aspect of godhead.

yagna: Vedic ritual involving chanting of hymns to invoke devas and offering of oblations into the fire altar so that the cosmos functions in one's favor.

Yaksha: Forest spirit associated with money and magic.

yantra: Sacred diagram.

Yellamman: Everybody's mother; village goddess whose head and body belong to different castes; goddess associated with ritual prostitution.

yoga: Mystical side of Hinduism; prevents the mind from being overwhelmed by the charms of the material world.

Yoni: Womb; female generative organ.

Bibliography

Abbot, J. E. and N. R. Godbole. *Stories of Indian Saints*. Delhi: Motilal Banarsidass, 1996.

Bhattacharji, Sukumari. *The Indian Theogony*. New Delhi: Penguin Books, 2000.

Coupe, Lawrence. *Myth*. London: Routledge, 1997.

Dange, Sadashiv Ambadas. *Encyclopaedia of Puranic Beliefs and Practices, Vol. 1–5*. New Delhi: Navrang, 1990.

Danielou, Alain. *Gods of Love and Ecstasy: The Traditions of Shiva and Dionysus*. Rochester, Vt.: Inner Traditions International, 1992.

——. *Hindu Polytheism*. Rochester, Vt.: Inner Traditions International, 1991.

Eliade, Mircea. *Myths, Dreams, and Mysteries*. London: Collins, 1974.

Flood, Gavin. *An Introduction to Hinduism*. New Delhi: Cambridge University Press, 1998.

Frawley, David. *From the River of Heaven*. Delhi: Motilal Banarsidass, 1992.

Graves, Robert. *The Greek Myths*. London: Penguin Books, 1960.

Hawley, J. S. and D. M. Wulff, eds. *The Divine Consort*. Boston: Beacon Press, 1982.

Highwater, Jamake. *Myth and Sexuality*. New York: Meridian, 1990.

Hiltebeitel, Alf, ed. *Criminal Gods and Demon Devotees*. Albany, N.Y.: State University of New York Press, 1989.

Hiltebeitel, Alf. *Cult of Draupadi, Vol. I*. Chicago: University of Chicago Press, 1988.

Hopkins, E. Washburn. *Epic Mythology*. Delhi: Motilal Banarsidass, 1986.

Jakimowicz-Shah, Marta. *Metamorphosis of Indian Gods*. Calcutta: Seagull Books, 1988.

Jayakar, Pupul. *The Earth Mother*. Delhi: Penguin Books, 1989.

Jordan, Michael. *Myths of the World*. London: Cambridge University Press, 1993.

Kinsley, David. *Hindu Goddesses*. Delhi: Motilal Banarsidass, 1987.

Klostermaier, Klaus K. *Hinduism: A Short History*. Oxford: Oneworld Publications, 2000.

Knappert, Jan. *An Encyclopedia of Myth and Legend: Indian Mythology*. New Delhi: HarperCollins, 1992.

Kosambi, Damodar Dharmanand. *Myth and Reality*. Mumbai: Popular Prakashan, Pvt. Ltd., 1994.

Kramrisch, Stella. *The Presence of Shiva*. New Delhi: Motilal Banarsidass, 1988.

Mani, Vettam. *Puranic Encyclopaedia*. Delhi: Motilal Banarsidass, 1996.

Martin-Dubost, Paul. *Ganesha: Enchanter of the Three Worlds*. Mumbai: Franco-Indian Research, 1997.

Mazumdar, Subash. *Who Is Who in the Mahabharata*. Mumbai: Bharatiya Vidya Bhavan, 1988.

Meyer, Johann Jakob. *Sexual Life in Ancient India*. Delhi: Motilal Banarsidass, 1989.

O'Flaherty, Wendy Doniger, trans. *Hindu Myths*. Delhi: Penguin Books, 1975.

———. *Origins of Evil in Hindu Mythology*. New Delhi: Motilal Banarsidass, 1988.

———. *The Rig Veda: An Anthology*. New Delhi: Penguin Books, 1994.

O'Flaherty, Wendy Doniger. *Sexual Metaphors and Animal Symbols in Indian Mythology*. New Delhi: Motilal Banarsidass, 1981.

———. *Śiva: The Erotic Ascetic*. London: Oxford University Press Paperbacks, 1981.

Panati, Charles. *Sacred Origins of Profound Things*. New York: Arkana, 1996.

Pandey, Rajbali. *Hindu Samskaras*. Delhi: Motilal Banarsidass, 1969.

Pattanaik, Devdutt. *Devi: An Introduction*. Mumbai: Vakil, Feffer and Simons, 2000.

———. *Goddess in India: Five Faces of the Eternal Feminine*. Rochester, Vt.: Inner Traditions International, 2000.

———. *Hanuman: An Introduction*. Mumbai: Vakil, Feffer and Simons, 2001.

———. *Man Who Was a Woman and Other Queer Tales from Hindu Lore*. New York: Harrington Park Press, 2001.

———. *Shiva: An Introduction*. Mumbai: Vakil, Feffer and Simons, 1997.

———. *Vishnu: An Introduction*. Mumbai: Vakil, Feffer and Simons, 1999.

Sen, Makhan Lal. *The Ramayana of Valmiki*. Delhi: Munshiram Manoharlal, 1978.

Subramaniam, Kamala. *Srimad Bhagavatam*. Mumbai: Bharatiya Vidya Bhavan, 1987.

Walker, Benjamin. *Hindu World, Vol. 1 and 2*. Delhi: Munshiram Manoharlal, 1983.

Wilkins, W. J. *Hindu Mythology*. Delhi: Rupa, 1997.

Zimmer, Heinrich. *Myths and Symbols in Indian Art and Civilization*. Delhi: Motilal Banarsidass, 1990.

Index

211